Motor Racing at Goodwood
An Illustrated History

INTERNATIONAL
GOODWOOD
MOTOR RACE MEETING
30th SEPT. 1950   START 2 p.m.

FOR TROPHIES & PRIZES
AWARDED BY THE

DAILY GRAPHIC

PHOTO BY L. KLEMANTASKI LTD.

Official Souvenir Programme **2/-**

BRITISH AUTOMOBILE RACING CLUB

Motor Racing at Goodwood
An Illustrated History

Robert Barker

breedon **books**
PUBLISHING

First published in Great Britain in 2002 by
The Breedon Books Publishing Company Limited
Breedon House, 3 The Parker Centre,
Derby, DE21 4SZ.

'Goodwood' and 'Festival of Speed'
are trademarks of The Goodwood Estate Company Limited.

ISBN 1 85983 282 2

Printed and bound by Butler & Tanner, Frome, Somerset, England.

Cover printing by Lawrence-Allen Colour Printers, Weston-super-Mare, Somerset.

Contents

Acknowledgements

I am grateful to Ted Walker of Ferret Fotographics for his help with the supply of the vast majority of the illustrations. In fact, all the pictures used are from Ted's glorious treasure-store unless they are otherwise credited. Although fewer in number, the images supplied by LAT Photographics are no less important. The proprietors of *The Autocar* have kindly given permission for the reproduction of the article by Tony Brooks. As always, my good friend Richard Page has acted as proof-reader. Patrick Barker and Stephen Payne were also kind enough to read through the original text. Their help has been invaluable but the errors which will inevitably sneak in are entirely my responsibility. Rupert Harding has been enthusiastic, helpful and ever-patient, for which I sincerely thank him. My interest in the history of racing at Goodwood has been sustained through the tolerance and kindness of the officers and staff of the British Automobile Racing Club. I thank their Chief Executive Mr Denis Carter and their ever-patient Press Officer Mrs Enid Smith for their patient help over so many years and for Mr Carter's kind permission to reproduce club material.

Prologue

'Bless my soul and what would the neighbours say?'

The Duke of Richmond and Gordon

THE BLACK YEARS of World War Two were followed by grey years of post-war austerity. Rationing continued as British industry toiled to revert to peacetime production after the all-out war effort. Those young men fortunate enough to return from war service found a country sapped by the effort and expenditure rather than the land fit for heroes which they deserved. Opportunities for relaxation and entertainment were few, and professional sport took time to get into its stride. While it did not take much imagination to improvise a football pitch, motor racing took rather more effort and outlay to arrange. Before the war, Brooklands, Donington and Crystal Palace had flourished, but Brooklands had gone for ever and many years would pass before the others would return to use.

Enthusiasm for motor sport had been boosted by the pre-war Donington Grands Prix and improvised events did take place in the early post-war years: hillclimbs, sprints, speed trials and even the odd race meeting on disused airfields. The Isle of Man and Jersey hosted real road racing, which was not permitted on the mainland, and this served to whet the appetite of the enthusiasts.

The Duke of Richmond and Gordon had been a racing driver and leading light of the Junior Car Club, one of the principle race organisers at Brooklands. The government had taken over agricultural land a short distance from his home, Goodwood House, to use as a satellite airfield linked to nearby Tangmere. Westhampnett airfield saw the arrival of 145 Squadron's Hurricanes in July 1940. During the following winter a hard perimeter road was built around the grass landing strips as poor drainage had proved a problem. Westhampnett was one of the busiest Battle of Britain airfields and Douglas Bader took off from there on his last mission. After hosting Spitfires and Typhoons, and units from America, Canada and Poland, the airfield closed in 1946.

Between sorties, pilots needed to relax. Squadron Leaders Tony Gaze and Dickie Stoop both had MGs and the RAF had some fuel that it would not miss. The resulting 'gentle dicing' around the perimeter road led Tony Gaze to approach the Duke of Richmond after the war and casually enquire 'When will we be having motor racing at Westhampnett?' The Duke was taken aback. He was inevitably involved with the effort to bring back motor racing but had never thought of bringing it to his own back yard.

Friends and experts were consulted and it was decided that the seemingly random design of a track for moving aircraft around boggy ground was in fact a fine race circuit with space for spectators and facilities, a happy coincidence that was compounded by the experience of the Goodwood staff in arranging major sporting events at the nearby horse racecourse. Other airfield circuits would emerge, but many made use of runways, which were flat and featureless by nature. Goodwood's perimeter road had some rise and fall to it, and provided a variety of corners and a fast straight. Westhampnett had been the name of the farm on which the airfield sat but 'Goodwood' was a name with an illustrious sporting history and was thus better suited to the new motor race circuit that was readied for the first meeting on 18 September 1948.

The Duke of Richmond and Gordon, Freddie to his friends, a man of great charm and many talents.

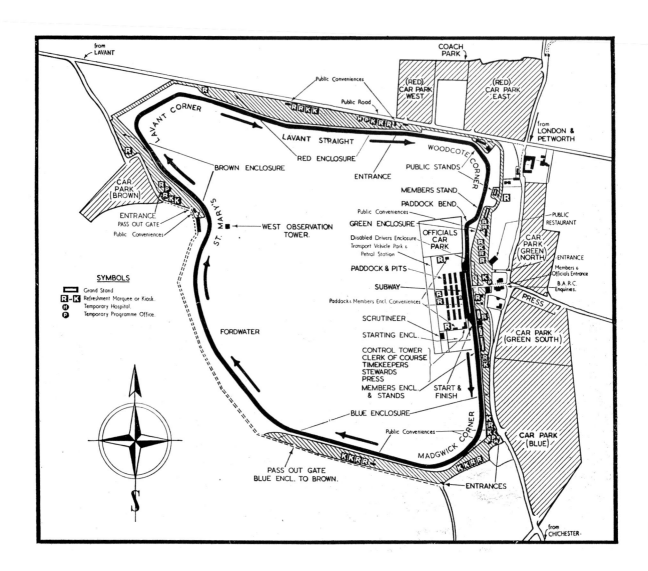

from
LAVANT

COACH
PARK

(RED)
CAR PARK
WEST

(RED)
CAR PARK
EAST

Public Conveniences

Public Road

R R K K

P P K R R R

from
LONDON &
PETWORTH

LAVANT CORNER

LAVANT STRAIGHT

WOODCOTE CORNER

RED ENCLOSURE

PUBLIC STANDS

ENTRANCE

MEMBERS STAND

BROWN ENCLOSURE

PADDOCK BEND

R

Public Conveniences

GREEN ENCLOSURE

R

PUBLIC
RESTAURANT

CAR
PARK
(BROWN)

R P
P
A R K K

Disabled Drivers Enclosure

OFFICIALS
CAR
PARK

CAR PARK
GREEN
NORTH

ENTRANCE
PASS OUT GATE

Transport Vehicle Park &
Petrol Station

R

R R R

ENTRANCE

Public Conveniences

ST. MARY'S

WEST OBSERVATION
TOWER.

PADDOCK & PITS

Members &
Officials Entrance

K

B.A.R.C.
Enquiries.

SUBWAY

R R

PRESS

Paddock & Members Encl. Conveniences

SYMBOLS

Grand Stand

R-K Refreshment Marquee or Kiosk.

H Temporary Hospital.

P Temporary Programme Office.

FORDWATER

SCRUTINEER

STARTING ENCL.

R

CAR PARK
(GREEN SOUTH)

CONTROL TOWER
CLERK OF COURSE
TIMEKEEPERS
STEWARDS
PRESS

MEMBERS ENCL.
& STANDS

START &
FINISH

BLUE ENCLOSURE

CAR PARK
(BLUE)

Public Conveniences

K K R R

MADGWICK CORNER

R R K
R

PASS OUT GATE
BLUE ENCL. TO BROWN.

K K R R

ENTRANCES

S

from
CHICHESTER.

1948

*'Goodwood was a great success –
we want more!'*

Bill Boddy, *Motor Sport*

THE FIRST meeting was an experiment. The site had been fenced and some facilities provided but the public could have only limited access as the RAF occupation was still in evidence. Nevertheless around 20,000 people arrived by car, bus, cycle and on foot to see the first racing on what would become a permanent race circuit on the UK mainland. The Brooklands' tradition of short races was revived, seven of the eight races being over three laps (under 8 miles) and the feature race over only five laps (12 miles).

Just five cars turned out for the opening race for closed cars: three Healeys, an HRG and the winner, Paul Pycroft's special-bodied SS100 Jaguar. The winner's speed was 66.42mph, and the race was over in about seven minutes. This may not seem a great adrenaline rush as we look over our shoulders from the sophisticated heights of 21st-century Formula 1, but think of those spectators in 1948. Enthusiasts had probably seen no racing for 10 years, and many of the crowd may have never before seen a car driven in competition. This was an experience either new or affectionately revived, and the crowd warmed to it.

The second race, for small sports cars, presented 12 starters and was won by Harry Lester's MG Magna from Peter Morgan's 4/4, with a mixture of pre-war Fiats, Rileys and others fighting for the minor places. George Phillips's Lester-modified MG TC won the next race, while the larger-engined sports car event went to Ken Watkins's BMW 328.

The race for 500cc cars was the only event in which all the entries were of

Spectators are restrained by their own common sense as Reg Parnell's Maserati 4CLT is chased by Bob Gerard's ERA at the opening meeting. *(18/9/48 Photo: LAT Photographic)*

post-war manufacture. The idea of economic miniature single-seaters powered by motorcycle engines had caught the imagination of the enthusiastic band of special builders although, even at this early stage, almost half the entry were Coopers. The small Surbiton concern was selling all the cars it could produce. Eric Brandon in the early Cooper managed to stall on the grid, allowing young Stirling Moss in the production version to storm into the lead. By the second lap he was so far ahead that his father signalled him to slow down. Once Brandon was under way he harried his way through to second place, but it was Moss who won, on the day after his 19th birthday. In his second season of competition he was already demonstrating the talent that would delight spectators for the next 14 years.

The last three races were for pure racing cars, the first falling to Dudley Folland's MG K3. The second brought out the cream of pre-war racers. Five ERAs were driven by Geoffrey Ansell (R9B), Graham Whitehead (R10B), John Bolster (R11B), George Nixon (R2A) and Peter Walker (R7B). Dennis Poore had the majestic Alfa Romeo 8C/35 and David Murray drove Parnell's Maserati 4CL. Nigel Mann and David Lewis both drove Alfa Romeo 8Cs with Chorlton's Bugatti and Richardson's ERA-engined Riley completing the field.

It was Poore who took the lead, with Walker and Bolster passing Nixon to challenge for first position. This spurred Poore to greater efforts, but Bolster provided the excitement in his efforts to pass Walker's ERA. They finished in that order with Bolster recording the fastest lap at 81.47mph.

The last and main race of the day brought back some of the cars from the previous event plus more ERAs for Cuth Harrison (R8C), Bob Gerard (R14B) and David Hampshire (R1A). Roy Salvadori brought out his Maserati 4C and Duncan Hamilton his Maserati 6CM, but the star attraction was Reg Parnell's new Maserati 4CLT on its first appearance in the UK. The national passion for the sport had propelled Italian motor racing back into its stride soon after the cessation of hostilities. Both Ferrari and Maserati produced new models at a time when shortages of both materials and fuel meant that the Britons were hard put to refettle their pre-war cars.

Thus Parnell's state-of-the-art machine stood out against the perpendicular cars of his rivals, though Gerard had put in the fastest lap in practice. Grid positions were determined by ballot rather than practice times and this system persisted longer at Goodwood than elsewhere. Duncan Hamilton took due advantage of his front-row position to take an initial lead, but Parnell was soon through to the front, followed by Hamilton, Hampshire, Gerard, Salvadori and Harrison. Soon Gerard, who rivalled Parnell as Britain's most successful post-war driver, was up to second place, and his efforts to take the lead kept the crowd on its toes. The Maserati was seen to be faster in a straight line but the ERA made up time in the corners. The scrap intensified over the last two laps with Gerard trying all he knew to find a way past. Parnell finally took the flag a mere 0.4 seconds ahead, to the cheers of the spectators who had had a thoroughly entertaining day to remember. Both they and the organisers went home happy, since a profit of around £1,000 crowned their efforts. The event was a success and Britain had a new race circuit.

Maserati 4CLT

Maserati carried forward the pre-war 4CL Maserati, building new examples in 1946. After the Maserati brothers left the business, development was carried on by Alberto Massimino. The four-cylinder 16-valve 1½-litre (78x78mm) engine gained two-stage supercharging. A twin-tube chassis frame resulted in a lower, smoother outline. There was new front suspension by upper rocker arms and coil springs, while at the rear it retained a live axle on leaf springs. The car won at its first outing, the 1948 San Remo Grand Prix, and took its name from the race. This model proved to be the backbone of Formula 1 racing until 1952 when the formula changed. Twenty cars were built and most were supplied to private teams. To Britain came 1595 (Leslie Brooke), 1596 (Reg Parnell) and 1598 ('B Bira'). Reg Parnell also owned 1593 (ex-Ascari) and other cars also changed hands. Two cars were supplied to the Argentine club for the use of their 'Drivers to Europe', Fangio and Campos. The model scored numerous victories, particularly during its early years. With the absence of Alfa Romeo, they enjoyed a good year in 1949 but, despite an updated version, the 4CLT/50, success was mostly found in the minor Formula 1 races, of which there were many around Europe. Their claimed 240bhp was below both Alfa Romeo and Ferrari, but what they lacked in power they made up for in numbers, availability and the support of the Maserati factory. The Ruggeri brothers used highly modified engines in two 4CLT/48s run under the Scuderia Milano banner and Enrico Plate later removed the superchargers from two 4CLT/48s, increased the capacity to two litres and used them for the new Formula 2 in 1952. Neither venture was a huge success.

Reg Parnell in his Maserati 4CLT is separated from the public by a small area of grass as he becomes the star of the opening meeting and the first King of Goodwood. (Photo: LAT Photographic)

Reg Parnell receives his trophy from the Duke of Richmond and Gordon and *Daily Graphic* (Kemsley Press) director Denis Berry.

Reg Parnell (1911–1964)

Derbyshire haulier and pig farmer Reg Parnell began racing in 1935. A serious accident at Brooklands involving Kay Petre cost him his competition licence, though it was reinstated on appeal. He began the construction of his own voiturette racer called the Challenger, though there was no time for its development. The war interrupted his career but he spent the time wisely buying all manner of laid-up racing machinery. After the war he was involved in an abortive attempt to buy a Mercedes Benz W154. He was Britain's most successful driver in the immediate post-war period, earning an invitation drive with the mighty Alfa Romeo team in the 1950 British Grand Prix, finishing a worthy third. He had most success driving his own cars, such as the Maserati 4CLT

and Ferrari 500/625, but he even tamed the troublesome BRM T15. He drove Rob Walker's B-type Connaught and Tommy Sopwith's Coopers. His years with Aston Martin built a relationship which culminated in his appointment as team manager in succession to John Wyer. As Aston Martin eased out of competition he set up the Yeoman Credit and Bowmaker teams. His own Reg Parnell Racing was in its early days when, in 1964, Reg died from peritonitis following a routine appendectomy. He was only 52.

The motor-racing world was shocked at the loss of a man who had done probably more than any other single driver to establish British motor racing after the war. At the dinner given in his honour on his retirement, Rodney Walkerley said 'We think of Stirling (Moss) with awe, Mike (Hawthorn) with admiration, but we think of Reg with affection. He is the prince of sportsmen.'

1949

PLANS FOR the following season were to set the pattern for the future. The authorities agreed to three major meetings at Easter, Whitsun and in September. The Easter International Meeting was to become the traditional curtain-raiser of the European season and, as the first major meeting of the year, often saw the debut of the latest racing machinery.

The 1949 event was no exception and the first race on the programme brought out the first Ferrari to race in the UK. Dudley Folland's 166 was joined by Peter Clark's single-seater HRG, John Heath's HW Alta and Ken Hutchison's Veritas. Jack Fairman's Riley held an early lead but the Ferrari came to the fore. Fairman also lost out to Frank Kennington in the ex-Harry Schell Cisitalia D46, who finished second.

The 500cc race was a disappointment for Stirling Moss, who retired his new Cooper after two laps. Lawrie Bond, creator of the Bond Minicar, had built his own 500cc car but got no further than the first corner where he left the road, running over photographer Guy Griffiths's cameras in the process. Austen May held the lead until the engine exploded in his Cooper – the actual car with which Moss had won at the opening meeting. 'Curly' Dryden led for the next three laps but slowed on the last lap and was caught by Stan Coldham's Cooper, which ran out the winner.

The Chichester Cup for supercharged racing cars over 1450cc brought back Reg Parnell in his Maserati, together with a similar car for Fred Ashmore. Both cars were entered by Scuderia Ambrosiana, an Anglo-Italian alliance which eased some of the problems of moving vehicles and funds around a Europe trussed up with regulations designed to make both activities difficult. Ken McAlpine appeared with the Maserati 8CM previously raced by Whitney Straight and Prince Bira. George Abecassis had the first Grand Prix Alta and Leslie Johnson an E-type ERA. Two E-types were made pre-war but had no opportunity to shine. It was Parnell who disappeared into the distance and won by almost 13 seconds from Dennis Poore's Alfa Romeo 8C/35, with Johnson's ERA E-type in third place.

Parnell put the lap record up to 86.40mph and did not improve on this in winning the feature race from Peter Whitehead's ERA (R10B) and Cuth Harrison's ERA (R8C). However, in winning the last of three handicap races from scratch, he increased the record to 87.10mph. The other handicaps were won by Kennington in the Cisitalia and Stirling Moss in his Cooper, the engine swapped from 500cc to 998cc JAP units.

> *'A really large assembly of spectators attended, and the racing, still to some extent experimental, can be written down as highly satisfactory'*
>
> Bill Boddy, *Motor Sport*

So Parnell had added three more victories to his Goodwood tally, but he would not be able to increase his score at Whitsun. Although the circuit had been improved during the winter, with grandstands at the start and at Woodcote corner, new enclosures at St Mary's and Madgwick corners and stronger fencing, the crowd pushed to the track's edge and some climbed onto advertising signs and buildings. The Duke of Richmond suspended racing and warned that the meeting would be abandoned if order was not restored. Fortunately the situation was resolved, but plans for the Whit meeting were cancelled to allow more time for safety improvements to be carried out.

There was a third event at Goodwood that year – the first of the meetings for members of the organising club, now called the British Automobile Racing Club. The intention was to give members a chance to race their own cars in a series of short races, many under handicap. Originally intended for sports cars only, single-seaters did appear in later years. Entries for the first of these meetings in August 1949 included one of the new Connaught sports cars. Two races were won by Eric Thompson in his lightweight HRG. His success with this car attracted entrants such as Rob Walker, Connaught and Aston Martin, who provided him with blue-blooded racing machines in which he demonstrated great skill. He was not willing to make racing a full time occupation, otherwise he would certainly feature more in the history of the sport.

The final meeting that year fell on Stirling Moss's 20th birthday and he obliged the press by winning the opening race for 2-litre racing cars in his Cooper JAP. Reg Parnell was back in his Maserati 4CLT and added the second race of the day to his already impressive score. Second was Peter Walker in an improving E-type ERA, but it should be remembered that these races were only over a mere 12 miles. Apart from the two Parnell Maseratis (the second driven by David Hampshire), the other entries were all of pre-war manufacture.

'Improvements in the form of covered stalls in the paddock, larger enclosures and covered stands were in evidence'
Bill Boddy, *Motor Sport*

There were new British racing cars in the offing, but these were yet to appear. The 500cc race saw a win by yet another of Britain's future stars, Peter Collins. His Cooper was fitted with a new overhead-camshaft Norton engine and he beat Dutchman Lex Beels by a second over five laps. Ken McAlpine (Maserati 8CM) won the first handicap, benefiting from a generous 34 seconds start over scratch man Parnell, who still managed to finish second.

The second handicap fell to Tony Rolt in the Alfa Aitken. This car had started life as the giant twin-engined Bimotore. One engine had been removed and, under the supervision of Freddie Dixon, the remaining motor had its supercharger removed and capacity stretched to 3440cc. The third handicap was won by Gordon Shillito's Riley.

The main race of the day for Formula 1 cars over 24 miles was sponsored by the *Daily Graphic*. Parnell and Hampshire in the two Maserati 4CLTs were joined by the older Maseratis of Joe Fry and Duncan Hamilton. The second E-type ERA was driven by Peter Walker, while older models of the marque were handled by Cuth Harrison (R8C), Brian Shawe-Taylor (R9B) and Bob Gerard (R14B). Rolt was out in the Alfa Aitken and Moss borrowed the works' Cooper JAP.

Richard Habershon had one of the famed Delage 15S8 cars. During the war, Reg Parnell had collected all the available Delage bits and pieces. The famous Dick Seaman car had remained more or less complete, the second car raced by Woodall had a new frame dating from its days with the Chula/Bira team and Habershon's car was assembled from remaining bits on another Chula/Bira frame with a new Parnell-made body.

Moss had drawn pole position in the ballot and took full advantage of the light weight and acceleration of the Cooper, leading from the flag. However, he was soon overhauled by the mighty horsepower behind him, and the JAP engine had had enough after two laps. Shawe-Taylor led Parnell and Gerard at the end of the first lap, but Parnell took the lead going into St Mary's on the second lap. Gerard moved up to second, but it was Peter Walker's E-type ERA that looked most threatening, passing Gerard and cutting Parnell's lead from three to one and a half seconds. Parnell took the hint and speeded up, matching his lap record in winning yet again. The final handicap race fell to Gerry Dunham's historic Alvis 12-70 Special of Brooklands memory.

Peter Walker drives
ERA E-type GP-1 to
second place behind
Reg Parnell's Maserati
4CLT in the five-lap
Woodcote Cup race.
(17/9/49)

Connaught L2

Rodney Clarke, proprietor of Continental Cars in Send, Surrey was joined after the war by Mike Oliver. Selling exotic cars and preparing racing cars for customers, they attracted one of those customers, Kenneth McAlpine of the famous building family, who backed them after they had set up Connaught Engineering. They bought chassis and engines from Lea Francis. The twin-cam 1767cc engines were considerably modified by Mike Oliver. New camshafts and pistons were fitted and, with Amal carburettors, 122bhp was claimed for the L2, the most popular model, three cars being built for McAlpine, Clarke and Oliver and three more for customers. P.L. Jonas and John Lyons (son of Sir William Lyons of Jaguar) opted for the standard L2, but Ken Downing chose the optional 1500cc engine and had his own, stark, bodywork made. The cars had some success but,

more importantly, they gave the team experience and encouraged them to develop the A-type Formula 2 car, also powered by a modified Lea Francis engine. Connaughts always insisted on a high standard of engineering and their cars were always beautifully built. This contributed to their downfall, construction methods at their F2 rivals Cooper being quicker and more flexible, though undeniably more 'agricultural'. The A-type F2 was followed by the B-type F1 car, which made its mark on history with Tony Brooks's win in the 1955 Syracuse Grand Prix. There were other minor successes for the likes of Archie Scott Brown and Stuart Lewis-Evans but, dogged by the lack of a first-class F1 engine and using modified Alta units, they were unable to sustain the heavy expenditure of maintaining a front-line racing team and sold up in October 1957. The GP cars continued racing in private hands but their time had passed. Mike Oliver became Folland's chief test pilot and Rodney Clarke died in 1979.

The Connaught L2 sports model of J. Beckwith-Smith at the Members' Meeting on 2 May 1953.

Bob Gerard in the cockpit of his rear-engined Cooper, still Bristol-powered and not a huge success.

Bob Gerard (1914–1990)

After trials driving in a Riley 9, Bob Gerard took to circuit racing at Brooklands and Donington, where he finished third in the 12-hour race. After the war he gathered together three ERAs and proved himself second only to Parnell as Britain's most successful driver, this despite his outdated machinery and decidedly short sight. Meticulous preparation had much to do with the old ERA's continued competitiveness and this applied to all the cars that he raced including a Cooper F3 and

Frazer Nash Le Mans Replica, both of which saw much success. 1953 saw him in a new Cooper Bristol T23 which he raced until 1956, often beating more exotic machines. 1957 saw him in a Cooper T43 with the Bristol engine from the old T23 (by now extended to 2246cc) rear mounted. This proved no match for the Climax-engined F2 cars and 'Mr Bob' gave up single-seater racing, though he continued racing Turner sports cars into the 1960s. He then became an entrant with Coopers for John Turner and later ran the quasi-works Merlyn F2 team.

1950

THE FIRST full season closed with Goodwood established alongside Silverstone as a regular venue for the burgeoning British motor-racing scene. Moving into a new decade, there was hope that the long-trumpeted BRM would soon be competing on equal terms with the established Grand Prix teams. The story is well known. Suffice to say that the production of a car of such advanced design during a time of such adversity, and under the direction of a committee, was always doomed to struggle if not to fail.

Adopting a radically different approach were the partners of Hersham and Walton Motors, John Heath and George Abecassis. The first car that they built, the HW Alta registered MPB77, had been sold to Tom Meyer, and they produced three cars, now known as HWM, intended for use either as sports racers or, with the removal of cycle wings and road equipment, as pure racing cars. However, they gave up their proposed entries at Le Mans to concentrate on what would become Formula 2 racing throughout Europe. While BRM struggled, HWM gave real international racing experience to the likes of Stirling Moss, Peter Collins, Lance Macklin and Duncan Hamilton. What is more, they were rarely seen as 'also rans', and alerted Europe to what was beginning in Britain.

Two of their new cars appeared in the first race at the 1950 Easter Meeting but, in the hands of Heath and Abecassis, both retired early. On the other hand, the Coopers with new JAP V-twin 1097cc engines were going well and Bill Aston took the victory ahead of Eric Brandon. The 500cc race attracted 23 entries (of which 20 started) indicating that the formula was now firmly established. The fact that 14 of the 23 entries were production cars bought from Coopers also shows the inevitable departure from the formula's original concept as motor racing on the cheap. In the absence of Moss it was to be 'Curly' Dryden's race, although Stan Coldham held the early lead. Though both were driving Coopers, there was a new car and driver in third place. Alf

Bottoms, speedway star, was developing his own car, the JBS, which would prove a worthy challenger to the established names.

The Chichester Cup for Formule Libre (literally 'free formula') cars saw Goodwood's first prestige foreign entry. Enrico Plate's Maserati 4CLTs were to be driven by Baron Emmanuel de Graffenried and the celebrated Siamese prince known as 'B Bira'. Against them were ranged the similar cars of Parnell and David Murray. Murray would later become famous as the man behind Ecurie Ecosse, the team from Edinburgh that won Le Mans not once, but twice. While Peter Whitehead non-started in the first Grand Prix Ferrari to reach these shores, at least the new HWMs were back out, this time with Abecassis and Moss at the helm. Duncan Hamilton's 6CM Maserati was joined by Roland Dutt's 8C and Poore's well-known Alfa. ERAs were driven by Graham Whitehead (R10B), Bob Gerard (R4A), Cuth Harrison (R8C) and Peter Walker in the E-type. John Rowley's Delage 15S8 completed the entry. Bira won from de Graffenried and Poore with Parnell only fourth. Was Parnell to be eclipsed at last or was he saving the machinery for the main race? Bira had quite a comfortable win but de Graffenried was harried all the way by Poore, who passed him on several occasions. The HWMs finished sixth and seventh, which was promising against the bigger cars.

Bill Aston scored his second win of the day in the first handicap race. The Richmond Trophy for Formula 1 cars (4500cc or 1500cc supercharged) brought back most of the eligible runners from the Chichester Cup plus Gordon Watson's Alta, Colin Murray's Maserati 6CM and Shawe-Taylor's ERA (R9B). Philip Fotheringham-Parker took over the Maserati that he shared with Duncan Hamilton. Bira slithered to the front from ninth on the grid, followed by de Graffenried and Parnell. The day had been bedevilled by a persistent drizzle, which now turned into heavy rain accompanied by gale-force winds. Bira evidently disliked the conditions, since he slowed and eventually stopped. Parnell, benefiting from a visor rather than goggles, passed de Graffenried and set off for home at a fair pace. As Bill Boddy of *Motor Sport* wrote: 'Parnell owed much to his 35/- visor, for both Bira and de Graffenried wore goggles, through which they just couldn't see in the rain'. Only four cars survived the ordeal but it was that man again who took the laurels from de Graffenried, Shawe-Taylor and Graham Whitehead. Two more handicaps finished the day, with Gerry Dunham and Duncan Hamilton victorious.

The second Members' Meeting took place on 6 May. No fewer than 10 races were scheduled, five from scratch and five under handicap. All events were over three laps and more than 100 entries were received. The scratch races were divided by engine size, two races for up to 1500cc, two up to 3000cc and one over 3000cc. Two handicap races were for MG cars only and the remaining three races mixed up the cars to add some variety. Early Cooper sports cars found themselves up against HRGs and Harry Lester's MG-engined special, which spawned a series of interesting sports-racers. Winners included Jim Mayer's 1500cc Lester MG (twice), Ken McAlpine's Connaught, Sydney Allard's Allard and Guy Gale's historic Darracq. Mrs Nancy Binns (Riley) recorded Goodwood's first win by a lady driver.

The Whit meeting of 1950 took place on the Saturday of the bank holiday weekend. The feature event was for the 500 International Trophy. Here was an attempt to raise the profile of 500cc racing to international level. Two seven-lap heats and a 15-lap final added up to a hard day's racing for these tiny motorcycle-engined machines, which were not renowned for their reliability over distance.

The international label was given credence by the presence of the Swedish Effyh team. Well-built and smartly turned out, these JAP-engined cars were equipped with both rollover bars and seat belts, compulsory in Sweden. Sadly, Ake Jonsson (Swedish champion), Eiler Svensson and Nils Gagner suffered plug maladies and all retired.

A rolling start was employed, perhaps to ease the strain on transmissions expected to cope with heavy demands. The first heat saw Paul Emery's front-engined Emeryson with a 200-yard lead, which ended with retirement on the second lap. Eric Brandon's Cooper took over and was chased to the flag by a young Peter Collins, who was among the drivers using Norton engines, which would eventually become essential equipment for these cars. Dennis Poore must have found the Cooper a very different proposition to his usual giant Alfa Romeo, but he managed third place ahead of that influential figure in future years, John Cooper.

The second heat fell to 'Curly' Dryden in another Cooper Norton, who then went on to win the final with 18-year-old Peter Collins little more than half a second behind. Poore's first experience of 500cc racing reached a spectacular conclusion when his fuel tank ignited as he was passing the pits. With considerable aplomb, he diverted to the paddock where the blaze was extinguished. The day was completed by three handicap races, two of which fell to Basil da Lissa's MG K3.

Two Members' Meetings filled the space between Whitsun and the final public meeting in September. Members' Meetings often included 10 or more short races, half of them under handicap. Races were not always hugely exciting and handicaps could be thoroughly confusing to the spectator. What is indisputable is the great benefit of these events to those who took part. The majority were weekend racers, often using a mildly tweaked road car. Some of these rarely if ever raced elsewhere, while other participants were ambitious hopefuls who put money, time and effort into their racing and some of whom would progress to the very highest levels of the sport. Perhaps the most famous of these was Mike Hawthorn, who entered his first race at Goodwood in June 1950 but failed to make the starting line on this occasion.

The September meeting brought a great deal of rain – and the BRM. It had taken five years for the concept to reach the race track. Its first appearance (at Silverstone) ended ignominiously when the transmission broke on the starting line. The car had been trumpeted loud and long and its failure received as much, if not more, publicity. The Silverstone car, chassis No.1 (actually the second frame built, the prototype being used for testing), was taken to Goodwood during the week preceding the race, where it tested successfully. French ace Raymond Sommer had the dubious honour of driving at Silverstone, but at Goodwood it was to be none other than Reg Parnell who would risk his reputation behind the wheel. In practice he lapped some 2.5 seconds inside his own lap record, but race day dawned grey and wet – and became steadily wetter.

The Woodcote Cup was a five-lap race for Formule Libre cars. Bira and de Graffenried were back again in Enrico Plate's Maserati 4CLTs and David Hampshire had his own. Belgian jazz-band leader Johnny Claes was in his yellow Talbot Lago T26C. The HWMs were back for Moss and Duncan Hamilton, while ERAs were handled by Peter Whitehead (R10B), his half-brother Graham Whitehead (R5B), Joe Ashmore (R1A) and Brian Shawe-Taylor (R9B). There were various Alfa Romeos for Dennis Poore (8C/35), Joe Goodhew (Tipo B) and Peter Walker (Rolt's Alfa Aitken). Completing the field was Forest Lycett's giant 8-litre Bentley driven by Leslie Johnson. From his second place on the grid, Parnell could see Peter Whitehead in pole position, while on his left was Ashmore's Maserati and, beyond him, Claes's Talbot Lago.

In clouds of steam and spray, the BRM, wheels spinning, eased off the line and was almost taken out from behind by Poore's giant Alfa Romeo, charging through from row four and swerving aside at the last moment. Bira and de Graffenried were ahead, but the pale green BRM passed them both on the first lap. Parnell used as much of the enormous power as he dared on the streaming wet road. Surging down the straight he drew away but, slowing for the corners, he was caught by Bira's more nimble Maserati. As we know, catching is not the same as passing, and the BRM howled round to record its maiden victory. A cheer rose from the sodden crowd and one can only imagine the feelings of Raymond Mays and Peter Berthon, who had struggled long and hard with the birth pains of their problem child, the BRM.

This had been a five-lap race, but the final event of the day was a 12-lap race. At under 30 miles, this was still no great test of reliability. The *Daily Graphic* Goodwood Trophy Race was for Formula 1 cars, and those eligible from the earlier race were supplemented by Duncan Hamilton's Maserati 6CM, Bob Gerard's ERA (R14B), Gordon Watson's Alta and Geoff

Richardson's home-built ERA-engined RRA. Parnell had a second-row grid position and again made a tentative start on the increasingly wet road. He was in the lead out of Madgwick corner and stayed there. Bira harried the BRM as before, later suggesting that the BRM had baulked him throughout the race. Nonetheless, Parnell won by some 12 seconds and the crowd, by now soaked to the skin, managed another cheer for this second victory. Raymond Mays commented: 'We were pleased with the success, although Peter [Berthon] and I knew that we still had only a half-developed car and that winning a couple of minor races at Goodwood had not put the BRM into the championship class'.

The press were once more heralding a great Grand Prix contender, but the more knowledgeable realised that everything was still to be proved. The V16 BRM won 18 races in the whole of its career and eight of these were in short Goodwood events. There was much sound and fury, and it is easy to say with hindsight that it signified nothing, but the effort and dedication involved should not be dismissed, even though it might have been better directed.

HWM partner John Heath with chassis FB102, second of the new single-seat Formula B cars. The car later crossed the Atlantic to become the Stovebolt Special. In the background is Joe Kelly's F1 Alta GP-3. *(10/4/50)*

Home-built but looking impressive is the JAP-engined Heath Special. Constructor and driver Cecil Heath finds no need of a crash helmet. *(10/4/50)*

Harry Lester, creator and designer of the Lester MG, drives it to fourth place in the 1500cc scratch race at the second Members' Meeting. *(6/5/50)*

Allards were popular at the early meetings. Here, at the second Members' Meeting, J.K.W. Baines is ahead of Peter Scott-Russell's Bentley. *(6/5/50)*

Brian Shawe-Taylor looks pensive as he awaits the start in ERA R9B. He was a fine driver whose career was cut short by a serious accident at Goodwood. *(27/5/50)*

Based on Lea Francis, Bill Skelly's Special was built to a very high standard. He managed sixth in the third Whitsun Handicap. *(27/5/50)*

BRM T15

Raymond Mays, who had fathered the ERA pre-war, was determined to produce a British world-beating Grand Prix car. Even before the war ended, Mays set about pursuing his British Racing Motor (BRM) ambition. He approached all and sundry in British engineering, begging for their support, both practical and financial. Meanwhile engineer Peter Berthon came up with an equally ambitious design involving a 1½-litre supercharged V16 engine with over 500bhp on tap. The Rolls-Royce aero-engine division was persuaded to provide the supercharger and industrialists throughout the land chipped in to aid the project. Management by committee resulted, which combined with the genuine difficulty in obtaining materials as well as funding in post-war Britain, meant that progress was painfully slow, and it was 1949 before the car first appeared. Then came its ignominious debut at Silverstone, followed by encouraging, if over-exaggerated, success at Goodwood. The car never became a world beater, though the highly individual scream of its engine was awesome and its enormous power brought respect from all who drove it. The later 'sprint' P30 version enjoyed an Indian summer in British Formule Libre racing, but BRM would eventually find international success with their first Grand Prix win in 1959 and Graham Hill's world championship in 1962.

Reg Parnell in the V16 BRM T15 on his victorious day, 30 September 1950. The road is streaming wet, as are the spectators behind Goodwood's trademark concrete barriers.

Jack Fairman in the Alfa Aitken, formerly the fabulous Bimotore, now reduced to a single engine. *(27/5/50)*

One of the pioneers of 500cc racing was IOTA. This Triumph-engined example was driven by Frank Aikens. In the background is Austen May's Cooper Norton Mk2. *(27/5/50)*

A rolling start for heat one of the 500 International Trophy race. Paul Emery (Emeryson) leads Peter Collins (Cooper), Eric Brandon (Cooper), Alan Brown (Cooper), John Cooper (Cooper) and the rest of the field. *(27/5/50 Author's collection)*

Clive Arengo produced several 500cc cars. This chassis had a Norton engine and the driver is Jim Bosisto. *(27/5/50)*

Finishing fourth in the Third Whitsun Handicap, John Green's Cooper T12 is powered by a 998cc Vincent HRD engine. *(27/5/50)*

Canadian Alvin (Spike) Rhiando developed his Trimax car to take 500cc, 750cc and 1100cc engines. The car was as flamboyant as its owner/driver. *(27/5/50)*

Peter Walker (1912–1984)

Another driver whose career was interrupted by the war, 'Skidder' Walker restarted post-war with his friend Peter Whitehead's ERA and challenged Raymond Mays and Bob Gerard on the hills before scoring two second places at Goodwood in the E-type ERA that few others had managed to tame. He was one of the first to tackle the BRM and earned a regular place in the works Jaguar team, for whom he won at Le Mans in 1951, driving with Peter Whitehead. He also finished second to Stirling Moss in that year's Tourist Trophy at Dundrod. In 1953 he was second at Le Mans and fourth in the Tourist Trophy, on each occasion co-driving with Stirling Moss. He moved to Aston Martin in 1955, sharing victory in the Goodwood Nine Hour Race with Dennis Poore. He again put in an impressive performance on the daunting Dundrod circuit, finishing fourth behind the works Mercedes. At the end of the 1956 season he retired from racing and disappeared from the public gaze.

Peter Walker brings E-type ERA GP-1 into the paddock followed by David Hampshire's Maserati 4CLT 1593.

1951

THE YEAR 1951 brought the Festival of Britain to London's South Bank and, with it, a sense that the gloom was at last lifting. The wonders of 3-D cinema were seen close by John Cobb's world land-speed record-holding Railton Mobil Special, both demonstrations of the skills to be found in the UK. At Goodwood the season began with the Easter meeting on 26 March. Bill Boddy wrote: 'The entry list was not outstanding, emphasising the bad effect which the rising cost of living is having on racing'.

The opening race saw one of the previous year's HWM Altas in the hands of new owner Oscar Moore, while two brand new genuinely single-seater works cars were handled by Stirling Moss and Lance Macklin. Ken McAlpine had the new A-series Connaught, a beautifully engineered single-seater with a Lea Francis derived engine, initially of 1767cc, but later enlarged to take advantage of the 2-litre limit in Formula 2. No fewer than seven Coopers were entered, powered either by JAP or Vincent HRD engines. Early leaders were the Coopers of Eric Brandon and Bill Aston, but it was Moss who came to the front on the final lap, with Macklin bringing the second HWM home fourth behind the two Coopers.

Alf Bottoms had not only developed his 500cc car, but also gone into limited production. Both he and 'Curly' Dryden drove Norton-engined examples, while Frank Aikens had a Triumph engine and Les Leston a JAP. There were also three Emerysons entered, though another star motorcyclist, Harold Daniel, non-started. The other two were driven by Paul Emery himself and, winner of the first-ever Goodwood race, Paul Pycroft. The majority of the 13 Coopers entered had Norton engines. Despite the presence of several of the latest Mk V Coopers, it was the JBS that dominated the race with Bottoms winning from Dryden. Ken Carter was third. Coopers were in the majority throughout the era of 500cc Formula 3, but they were not always dominant. JBS and Kieft in particular stole their thunder on numerous occasions.

The Chichester Cup Formule Libre race featured a new marque – OSCA. The Maserati brothers sold their eponymous company and moved to Bologna, where they developed their own range of sports racing and formula cars under the name of 'Officine Specializate Construzione Automobili'. Amedee Gordini had designed a 4½-litre engine for Formula 1, but could not afford to produce it. OSCA took over the design and adapted it to fit the Maserati 4CLT chassis. Prince Bira had his own car modified in this way, hoping to extend its useful life. Unmodified 4CLTs were ranged against him, driven by David Murray and Reg Parnell, though the cars of David Hampshire and John James did not start. ERAs were driven by Bob Gerard (R14B), Fred Ashmore (probably R7B), Graham Whitehead (R10B), Brian Shawe-Taylor (R9B), Philip Fotheringham-Parker (R5B) and John Green (R2A). Johnnie Claes had his yellow Talbot Lago T26C and Joe Goodhew his Alfa Romeo Tipo B. As all were entered for the feature race later in the day, there seemed no point in over-stressing the machinery and the race proved something of a procession, with little passing. Parnell won from Shawe-Taylor with Bira third.

The 12-lap Richmond Trophy saw rather more excitement, with Parnell hounding the OSCA for the first two laps until the Maserati spun off out in the country, narrowly avoiding a haystack. Rejoining in fifth place Parnell took two laps to get back up to second but after only two more laps a detached oil scavenge pump pipe put him out of the race. Shawe-Taylor hung on to second place ahead of Duncan Hamilton (in ERA R5B which he shared with Fotheringham-Parker) with Claes fourth and Moss a worthy fifth in the 2-litre HWM.

On 14 April *Motor Cycling* magazine organised the only motorcycle meeting to be held at Goodwood. The meeting would seem to have been a success but was not repeated. Geoff Duke won the main race on his Norton from Bill Doran's works AJS and Dickie Dale's Norton. Bill Boddice took the sidecar event with Geoff Duke again succeeding in the 350cc race.

The fifth Members' Meeting on 21 April 1951 saw the debut of John Michael Hawthorn, driving his father Leslie's Riley Ulster Imp. In the first race of the day he finished third, improving to second in his handicap event.

The Whitsun meeting again featured the 500cc cars and brought the first appearance of Stirling Moss in the new Kieft Norton. Its only previous running had been a few trial laps in the rain at Brands Hatch. Nobody noticed the resulting rust on the throttle cable and this slowed Moss in the first heat. After moving up from sixth on the grid to second on the road, he was forced to drop back to ninth, just qualifying for the final. The winner of the first heat was Eric Brandon, long-time friend of John Cooper. One of motor racing's characters, Jimmy Richmond, had brought together Brandon and Alan Brown to race new Mk V Coopers under the name of Ecurie Richmond as a quasi works team.

The 500cc movement was not short of characters. Third behind Jack Westcott came George Wicken, whose Cooper bore the legend *'C'est si bon'*, although it would be a few years later that Ian Raby's car would display the graphic description 'Puddle Jumper'.

Piero Taruffi was missing from the second heat. As this was his first appearance at Goodwood he had to complete three practice laps under observation, but engine trouble stopped him a quarter of a lap short. It seems terribly hard that a driver of his international repute should have been excluded thus, but the stewards decided that the rules could not be bent. Alan Brown gave Ecurie Richmond its second win and Mr Bernard Ecclestone 'drove brilliantly' (according to one report) into second place. Though none of the other drivers have quite reached Bernie's level of success, there were other notables in the entry list. This may have been a junior racing formula but many of the best drivers of the time competed. Ken McAlpine, Bob Gerard, Harry Schell and Johnny Claes were all racing at Goodwood that day, vying with the half-litre regulars.

While the diminutive single-seaters were getting their breath back the crowd was treated to two heats of the Festival of Britain Trophy Race for Formule Libre cars. Another important figure strode onto Goodwood's stage in the brisk and imposing form of Guy Anthony Vandervell, founder of bearing manufacturers Vandervell Products Ltd. An early and ardent supporter of the BRM project, he had tired of the delays and frustrations and bought one of Mr Ferrari's products, to get some practice before developing his own machine 'to beat those bloody red cars'. His first Ferrari, bought in 1949, had been sent back to Modena as unsatisfactory. The second car, a long wheelbase 125 model, was raced once in 1950 and then sent back to have the 1½-litre supercharged engine exchanged for the newer 4½-litre unsupercharged Grand Prix unit. In this form it had won a famous race at Silverstone a couple of weeks earlier. In a rainstorm of monsoon proportions, the race had been abandoned after six laps with the Thin Wall Special (as the car was known) leading ahead of the works Alfa Romeo team. It will come as no surprise that the driver was Reg Parnell, who was once again at the wheel at Goodwood.

Ranged against him in the first heat were ERAs for Bob Gerard, Brian Shawe-Taylor, Graham Whitehead and Claude Hamilton, Maserati 4CLTs for Baron de Graffenried and David Murray, Tony Rolt in Rob Walker's ERA-engined Delage and Duncan Hamilton's Talbot Lago amongst others. Parnell made the big Ferrari look easy to drive. His race average was below Bira's lap record, and Parnell set a new lap record at 93.10mph. Second man de Graffenried was some 13 seconds behind after only seven laps.

The second heat brought together Bira's OSCA and the Maseratis of world champion Giuseppe Farina, Harry Schell, David Hampshire and Ken

McAlpine. It was Dennis Poore's mammoth Alfa Romeo 8C/35 which led from the start, with Bira and Farina snapping at his heels. Poore waved them past but the road was just not wide enough. Bira eventually squeezed past but Farina, not perhaps the most patient of drivers, waved menacingly from the cockpit until he finally took second place on lap three. Bira was not to be caught, but his oil scavenge pump was damaged, leading to his first lap retirement in the final.

Before that final the 500cc cars came out to complete their event. The Ecurie Richmond Coopers had dominated the heats and were favourites for the final. However, the Kieft's throttle cable had been de-rusted and Moss was able to demonstrate its true potential. In a race of 15 laps he drew out a lead of 22 seconds and broke the class lap record. Alan Brown was second but Eric Brandon was slowed with a mechanical problem and finished fifth.

The final of the the Festival of Britain Trophy was won, almost inevitably, by Reg Parnell in the Thin Wall. For the first six laps it looked like a walkover, but then Farina shook off the following pack and pushed Parnell into setting yet another lap record at 94.53mph. The cut and thrust continued right through the field with de Graffenried duelling with Shawe-Taylor, Hamilton with Rolt and Fotheringham-Parker with Whitehead.

Both the June and August Members' Meetings brought more success to young Mike Hawthorn driving his father's Riley TT Sprite. His run of victories was enough to secure him the *Motor Sport* Brooklands Memorial Trophy, awarded for points scored at the season's Members' Meetings.

The final event of 1951 brought an effective end to the first post-war Grand Prix formula of 1½-litre supercharged or 4½-litre unsupercharged engines. Although the formula was not due to change until 1954, the retirement of Alfa Romeo left only Ferrari and BRM as front-line contenders. With BRM still not seen as reliable opposition to the Italians, it was decided to race for the world championship under Formula 2, with a 2-litre unsupercharged or 500cc supercharged limit.

And so it was something of a last hurrah that brought 1950 world champion Giuseppe Farina back to the circuit, but this time with a works Alfa Romeo 159. This was not the very latest machine but a car with a rear swing axle. Nonetheless, it was the first time that Reg Parnell was truly eclipsed at Goodwood by a superior car and driver. BRM had stayed at Monza to test after the Italian Grand Prix, leaving Parnell free to drive the Thin Wall in place of Alberto Ascari, whose son had been taken ill in Italy. That Farina could beat Parnell by seven seconds in the five-lap Woodcote Cup libre race demonstrates the enormous power of the Alfa, Farina setting a new record at 96.92mph. Third, over half a minute behind the Thin Wall, came Tony Rolt in Rob Walker's ERA-engined Delage.

This was to be the British public's first opportunity to see Jaguar's C-type, which had scored a brilliant victory at Le Mans. Stirling Moss galloped away with the sports car race ahead of a host of racing Jaguar XK120s and Frazer Nash Le Mans Replicas. In the following handicap race, Mike Hawthorn blotted his copy book with an off-road excursion and could only finish 11th and last. Despite starting from scratch, Moss won the second handicap race, leaving the sports car lap record at 86.02mph.

The third handicap gave Farina the chance to equal the overall lap record at 96.92mph. Starting from scratch, he powered through the field to fourth place at the start of the final lap. He overtook Tony Rolt in the ERA Delage, caught George Abecassis's HWM at the approach to Woodcote and came out of the last corner on the tail of Stirling Moss. In the blast to the line he passed the second HWM to win by two seconds.

The third car to bear the name Lotus appeared in the fourth handicap, but its creator Colin Chapman retired after two laps.

The final race, the *Daily Graphic* Trophy for Formula 1 cars, saw the Alfa out once more and Farina at his boldest. Parnell led briefly in the Thin Wall but Farina was soon ahead, driving faster than he had in the earlier races. He won by over seven seconds and left the lap record at 97.36mph. As he blasted across the finish line in front of the pits and the crowded enclosures, the officials were conscious of the potential dangers. It was subsequently decided to slow the cars at this point on the circuit and the chicane (or, to be exact, Paddock Bend) was inserted between Woodcote corner and the finish line. This was to become one of the most familiar places on the circuit and a most popular viewing point.

At All Events-

Leading All the Way

DAILY GRAPHIC
DAILY & SKETCH

Saturday, September 29, 1951 — GOODWOOD EDITION

His cornering will thrill the crowds

Stirling Moss acknowledges cheers of the crowd who were thrilled by his spectacular cornering.

SPEED ACES IN BATTLE FOR TROPHY

By KAY PETRE, *Daily Graphic* Motoring Correspondent

MOST spectacular and sizzling battle for the "Daily Graphic" Trophy race will be fought to-day between Europe's ace drivers on the world's fastest cars, and Goodwood champion Reg Parnell, who will defend his title on a BRM.

Nerves and skill will be strained to the limit to beat the "unbeatable" Reg, who has won the DAILY GRAPHIC Trophy three times and keeps the Trophy Cup. A new cup is being presented at this meeting.

Alberto Ascari, newcomer to Goodwood.

FOUR YEARS OF HARD WORK GOT STIRLING MOSS TO THE TOP

TWENTY-TWO-YEAR-OLD Stirling Moss—twice winner of the T.T.—who has rocketed to the top in four race-packed years, has come up the driving ladder the hard way.

Moss began on a small Cooper 500 in 1947. He took in as many hill climbs, speed sprints and short races for 500c.c. cars as he could.

In 1948 he added a 1,000c.c. engine that was interchangeable with the 500c.c. unit, and drove in every race in Britain that would accept him.

In September of that year he won his first Goodwood race on a 500c.c. Cooper at 71.92 m.p.h.

He decided to make driving his profession.

With his father he went on the Continent in 1949, and as he always put up a good show race promoters offered him reasonable starting money, but it was still a long way from being a "living wage."

His first big chance came when John Heath chose him to drive in the newly formed H.W.M. team with young Lance Macklin.

His greatest achievement was winning the T.T. in 1950 in blinding rain at Belfast. He had "arrived."

This year Jaguar's booked him as number-one driver for Le Mans, and the T.T.—which he won a second time.

B.R.M.'s invited him to drive for them. Race promoters invited him to drive his H.W.M. in grand prix races.

And the Italians have shown a big interest in trying him on their cars.

Famous drivers

A newcomer to this circuit is Italy's brilliant young driver Alberto Ascari, who enters the fray on Tony Vandervell's "Thinwall" Ferrari special—the car that holds the Goodwood lap record at 94.54 m.p.h. set up at Whitsun by . . . Parnell.

Other famous drivers who will line up for the 15-lap scratch Trophy race will be Brian Shawe - Taylor, ERA, Bob Gerard, ERA, Stirling Moss and George Abecassis, H.W.M.'s, all experienced grand prix drivers.

Breath-taking speeds and unbelievably fast cornering will be seen. New records will be set up and the finest driving ever to be seen at Goodwood will take place to-day on this star-studded field.

Watch how the fast drivers approach a corner, cut off at the same spot, and slide the car around in a four-wheel drift.

Those old records seem so slow now

Thousands at Goodwood to-day will remember with nostalgia the pre-war racing years when cars hurtled around Donington, and Brooklands Mountain and Campbell circuits at what looked like terrific speeds.

Compare the lap records of those tracks with to-day's speeds on the Goodwood circuit and they sound slow and tame. The famous pre-war German Auto Union and Mercedes never bettered 85.62 m.p.h. on Donington. The lap record on Brooklands Mountain circuit is 84.31 m.p.h., the Campbell circuit 77.79 m.p.h., while Crystal Palace was only 60.97 m.p.h. The Goodwood lap record, set up in a race by Reg Parnell at Whitsun, stands at 94.54 m.p.h.

Miniature newspaper produced by the *Daily Graphic.* Alberto Ascari was a non-starter on the day. *(29/9/51 Author's collection)*

Early Cooper sports cars include this Rover-engined example, driven here in the seventh Members' Meeting by E.M. Mackay. *(18/8/51)*

Start of the *Daily Graphic* Goodwood Trophy. Reg Parnell (Thinwall Special) gets away ahead of Nino Farina's Alfa Romeo 159, Brian Shawe-Taylor's ERA and Tony Rolt's ERA-Delage. *(29/9/51 Author's collection)*

Jaguar XK120C

William Lyons's Swallow Sidecars changed its name to Jaguar in 1945, the initials SS having attained a whole new meaning. Before the car came the engine, 3442cc straight-six 'XK'. First it powered the XK120 (capable of 120mph), a two-seater sports car launched in 1948 and selling for £1,300 to a market starved of performance cars of any sort, let alone one of delightful proportion. The works raced these cars, including a try-out at Le Mans. Convinced of the commercial value of a win in the classic French race, William Lyons commissioned the C-type competition model with the engine modified to give 210bhp in a multi-tubular space frame. Malcolm Sayer designed a smooth body in 18swg aluminium. Front suspen-

sion was similar to the XK120, independent by wishbones and torsion bars, but the rear was by Salisbury axle and trailing links. The car first appeared at Le Mans in 1951, three cars starting, two retiring and the third winning, driven by Peter Walker and Peter Whitehead. Jaguar was famous overnight and never looked back. The C-type had an illustrious competition career including a second Le Mans win in 1953. Private entrants gradually got their hands on production versions and the car was seen both at home and abroad for many years in racing at all levels. It spawned a worthy successor in the D-type, which had an even better record at Le Mans. There can be no doubt that Jaguar's reputation was greatly enhanced by its competition successes, not least those of the XK120C.

Beautifully presented as always is the Ecurie Ecosse C-type Jaguar at the Nine Hours Race of 1953. *(Author's collection)*

Giuseppe Farina is seen here in the cockpit of an Alfa Romeo at the 1950 British Grand Prix.

Giuseppe Farina (1906–1966)

Doctor of political economy and member of the famed coachbuilding family, 'Nino' Farina gave up a career as a cavalry officer to pursue his passion for motor racing. Coming to the attention of Tazio Nuvolari, he was Italian champion in 1937 and 1938 and progressed to become Alfa Romeo team leader by 1939. National champion again in 1939, he was called upon once more by Alfa Romeo when the Alfetta was brought out again in 1946. After driving Maseratis and Ferraris, he returned to Alfa Romeo in 1950 as one of the mythical 'Three F's': Fangio, Fagioli and Farina. A brilliant year saw him win the inaugural World Drivers' Championship. 1951 was not so successful and, with Alfa Romeo's withdrawal in 1952, he joined Ferrari. He was not at ease as number two to Ascari, who became world champion that year. He had a better year in 1953 and became Ferrari number one in 1954 when Ascari left for Lancia. A bad crash in the Mille Miglia was followed by a worse accident at Monza in which he was badly burned. He raced again with the help of pain-killing injections in 1955, but he retired before the year's end. Two unsuccessful sorties to Indianapolis provided a postscript to a long and turbulent career. Known as an unyielding competitor given to displays of temperament, he spent his remaining years in the motor business until his Lotus Cortina slid off an icy road into a telegraph pole at Chambéry in France.

1952

'Goodwood is, not surprisingly, my favourite British circuit'
Mike Hawthorn

1952 saw the suspension of Formula 1 as the championship formula. Raymond Mays did not intend to pack his BRMs away and the next two years saw continued domestic rivalry with Tony Vandervell's Ferrari Thin Wall Special.

Young dental student Tony Brooks had persuaded his mother that a Healey Silverstone would make a sensible shopping car. It also provided him with a car for club racing and he took his place on the grid at the Members' Meeting in March 1952. Matched against him was Arthur Hely in the ex-Lady Mary Grosvenor Frazer Nash Le Mans Replica. Mr Hely was impressed by young Brooks over the course of the 1952 season and arranged for him to drive the Frazer Nash in 1953. This led to a works Frazer Nash drive and to that history-making victory with a Connaught in the Syracuse Grand Prix of 1955.

Mike Hawthorn continued his winning ways at the season's first Members' Meeting. Meanwhile, Bob Chase, a family friend, was at the Cooper Car Company in Surbiton ordering a new front-engined single-seat Formula 2 car powered by the 2-litre Bristol engine. Coopers laid down an initial run of four cars, two for Ecurie Richmond's Eric Brandon and Alan Brown, one as a works car (subsequently sold to Archie Bryde) and one for Chase. Four or five more cars would be built during the year. The Chase-owned car would be prepared at Farnham's Tourist Trophy Garage by Leslie Hawthorn. All four Cooper Bristol T20s were entered for the opening race at the Easter meeting on 14 April.

Connaught's Lea Francis based engines had been increased to 1960cc, but the first two cars, driven by Ken McAlpine and Downing, suffered engine failure in practice and Bill Black's car (driven by Philip Fotheringham-Parker) non-started to avoid a similar oil pump failure. The latest version of the HWM with George Abecassis at the wheel recorded second-fastest practice time but retired early in the race. Archie Butterworth created a flat-four air-cooled engine for which Bill Aston had Coopers produce a chassis. Two examples of the resulting Aston Butterworth were built but neither was consistently quick.

The establishment was rocked when Hawthorn set the fastest practice lap, and pulverised when he won the race, leaving the Richmond cars to fight over second place. The winning margin of 22 seconds was evidence of young Hawthorn's talent, but also of Hawthorn senior's skill with tuning and knowledge of nitro-methane fuels. The fourth Cooper Bristol, to be driven by John Cooper, non-started in this first race probably in order to preserve it for the Chichester Cup Formule Libre race. None other than the great Juan Manuel Fangio had agreed to take the wheel.

Pausing just long enough for Stirling Moss to win the Formula 3 race in his Kieft, the main protagonists were wheeled out again for the Chichester Cup libre event. Bob Gerard, Ken Wharton and Graham Whitehead had ERAs, Tony Rolt the ERA Delage, Dennis Poore his Alfa Romeo 8C/35. Joe Kelly drove his GP Alta, while Gordon Watson piloted his new Formula 2 model. Bobbie Baird's Maserati 4CLT had been much modified with a new chassis and body and was now known as the Baird Griffin. The Thin Wall Special was driven by test driver Ken Richardson but did not survive the first lap. Against this assembled might, Hawthorn again took pole position and was never passed. Tony Rolt was second in the ERA Delage, Philip Fotheringham-Parker brought the Talbot Lago he shared with Duncan Hamilton home third, Poore was fourth in the Alfa and Sydney Allard in his Cadillac-engined J2X kept Fangio in sixth place.

Hawthorn was impressive. His second win confirmed the first to be no fluke, but the chance of a third looked remote as the Thin Wall was handed over to Froilan Gonzalez. It was the Argentinian ace who took the large Ferrari by the scruff of its neck and power-slid to a convincing win. However Hawthorn was unchallenged in second place while Duncan Hamilton was third in his Talbot Lago, looking somewhat like Gonzalez in style.

This had been a dramatic debut on the international motor racing scene. By the end of the following year, Hawthorn would be a works Ferrari driver with a Grand Prix win to his credit, and in 1958 he would become the first British world champion. Between these events, the British press would stir up a storm about Hawthorn missing National Service, the compulsory conscription to the armed forces which faced all young men at this time. It was not widely appreciated that he suffered from a serious liver complaint which would have exempted him and would also have shortened his life, which, as it transpired, was cut short by a tragic road accident on the Guildford bypass in 1959.

The Formula 3 event at Whitsun fell to Bob Gerard in a Cooper, while the Formule Libre race was won by Mike Hawthorn. It was significant that this was a race which it had been intended to run as two heats and a final. A poor entry saw it reduced to a single 15-lap race. Though Gerard was second in his ERA and Poore's Alfa was third, these cars were getting decidedly long in the tooth, had lost the arena of international Formula 1 racing and were being seen off by modern 2-litre cars. Although Formule Libre races would continue to give them exercise for some time to come, they were being edged out by the new generation.

The Members' Meetings were seeing much success by the Frazer Nash Le Mans Replicas, Tony Crook being challenged by Lawrence Mitchell and Rodney Peacock, names largely forgotten today but consistent performers in their day. Jaguar XK120s were equally successful in the larger capacity class, with drivers like Jim Swift, Duncan Russell, Bill Holt, Stanley Boshier and Michael Head, father of Williams designer Patrick.

At Le Mans, sports cars raced non-stop for 24 hours, but the UK had never seen night racing. The BARC came up with the bold notion of a race starting at 3pm and running for nine hours till midnight. Works support from Jaguar and Aston Martin brought out a good crowd, despite the threat of wet weather. The best British drivers of the day were engaged. The works C-type Jaguars were shared by Stirling Moss/Peter Walker, Tony Rolt/Duncan Hamilton and Peter Whitehead/Ian Stewart. Aston Martin's drivers were Reg Parnell/Eric Thompson, George Abecassis/Dennis Poore and Peter Collins/Pat Griffith. There were private Ferraris for Bobbie Baird/Roy Salvadori and Tom Cole/Graham Whitehead and a Talbot T26GS for Philippe Etancelin/ Pierre 'Levegh' (Bouillon). The winners were likely to be found among this group and Frazer Nash and Lester were likely contenders for the smaller capacity classes.

The cars lined up in race number order in echelon formation in front of the new pit building. The drivers waited on the opposite side of the road and sprinted to their cars on the starter's order. As usual, Moss was first to his car, but Rolt led at the end of lap one. By lap five the faster cars had begun to lap the slowest. After an hour it was Goodwood favourite Parnell in the lead from Rolt, Abecassis and Moss. Peter Whitehead's Jaguar left the road at Madgwick and retired shortly after, as did the Talbot.

After the first driver changes, smoke was seen coming from the back axle of Eric Thompson's Aston Martin. The DB3 was brought into the pits and, as it was refuelled, several gallons slopped over the rear of the car and immediately ignited. Team manager John Wyer was leaning into the cockpit and suffered burns serious enough to keep him out of action for six weeks. The drivers escaped unhurt, but two of the mechanics, Jack Sopp and Fred Lownes, were not so lucky. Parnell, having lost his car, took over as Aston team manager, only to learn that Poore had lost all but top gear. Abecassis took over but was delayed when first the starter jammed and then there were no gears at all to be found. He eventually stuttered away in top gear but this meant that Astons were effectively reduced to one car.

By half distance, the Jaguars of Moss/Walker and Rolt/Hamilton led the Collins/Griffith Aston with the two Ferraris closing in, Salvadori ahead. As lights were switched on and the luminous paint on the kerbing began to glow, the Jaguars had a cushion of some five laps over the Ferrari, which had moved up to third. Then fate struck at the Jaguars as a half shaft failed on the Rolt/Hamilton car, moving Salvadori up to second place, albeit five laps behind the Moss/Walker car. Then half an hour later the leading Jaguar toured into the pits with a broken rear axle locating arm. The valiant mechanics embarked on repairs, but the job took a whole hour. This left the Baird/Salvadori Ferrari a lap ahead of the Collins/Griffith Aston Martin, which was three laps ahead of the Cole/Whitehead Ferrari.

The leading Ferrari came in for its last pit stop. At the wheel change, the jack sank into Tarmac softened by the Aston fire. Then the car would not start – the battery was flat. Gregor Grant, writing in *Autosport*, wrote: 'At 10.23pm Salvadori came in to refuel and hand over to Baird. The Belfast man pressed the starter, there was a click – and silence!' The delay in finding a spare battery and jump leads cost four laps.

Bobbie Baird shot out of the pits for a single lap, returning to let Salvadori get behind the wheel again. In his eagerness, Salvadori spun and stalled at Woodcote and was penalised one lap for the resulting push start.

And so the Aston Martin was in the lead and stayed there till midnight, with the two Ferraris finishing next in the order Cole/Whitehead and Baird/Salvadori. Moss brought the sole surviving Jaguar home fifth to win his class, with the Jim Mayers/Mike Keen Lester sixth and winners of the 1500cc class. In fact, the three 'Monkey Stable' Lesters finished in the first three places in their class and won the team prize. The event was regarded as a great success by the motor racing establishment but the public at large was not so enthusiastic and neither was the local population.

The Nine Hours Race did not replace the September meeting, which brought back Giuseppe Farina, this time as driver of the latest Thin Wall Special Ferrari 375, opposed by no fewer than three works BRMs for Gonzalez, Parnell and Wharton. Mike Hawthorn was suffering one of his sporadic bouts of illness. His place in the Cooper Bristol was to have been taken by Duncan Hamilton, but the car broke in practice. There remained a very full grid for the Madgwick Cup Formula 2 race, with Bill Dobson driving the Scuderia Ambrosiana Ferrari 125, a Ferrari 500 for Salvadori, the Richmond Cooper Bristols for Brandon and Brown and works Connaughts for Poore, Thompson and McAlpine with Downing and Marr in their own cars. Ecurie Ecosse, the famed Scottish sports car team, had branched out into single-seater racing with a Cooper Bristol for Ninian Sanderson. Other Cooper Bristols were driven by John Barber and Andre Loens. Bill Aston was back with the Aston Butterworth and there were new Formula 2 Altas for Peter Whitehead, Gordon Watson and Oliver Simpson. Frazer Nash had produced single-seaters based on the Le Mans Replica for Ken Wharton and Bill Skelly. Yet another car new to the 1952 season was the G-type ERA with Stirling Moss engaged as driver. Formula 2 was certainly proving a success, encouraged by its championship status. Moss was eliminated in a first lap accident as was Loens. Downing and Poore scored a 1-2 for Connaught, with Brown's Cooper third.

> '*Goodwood was looking at its best; although a cold wind blew over the circuit, there was sufficient sunshine to provide the Technicolour effects for which the Sussex venue is renowned*'
> Gregor Grant, *Autosport*

Moss made up for his disappointment with a win in the 500cc race by just over a second from Les Leston.

Most of the Formula 2 runners returned for the libre race, but it was the BRM of Gonzalez that led Farina's Thin Wall and Parnell's BRM. Wharton's BRM failed at the start and the best of the rest was Alan Brown's Cooper Bristol.

Hawthorn's place in the works Jaguar C-type was taken by Tony Rolt. He was opposed by Moss in the private car of Tommy Wisdom. Moss broke the lap record but could not catch the Rolt car with the latest works tweaks.

The handicap races fell to Tony Gaze in the ex-Straight/Bira Maserati 8CM and Bill Dobson in the Ecurie Ecosse Jaguar XK120.

The 15-lap *Daily Graphic* Trophy started without Farina as the Thin Wall stripped the crown wheel on the last lap of the libre race. This left the BRMs with little effective opposition and they finished 1-2-3 in the order Gonzalez, Parnell, Wharton – the only clean sweep ever by the V16 cars. Raymond Mays said of the achievement 'This was the result for which we had waited so long. It had come too late.'

Frazer Nash Le Mans Replica Mark II

In 1948 Frazer Nash introduced their 'High Speed' model, a two-seat traditional sports car with cycle wings, powered by the Bristol 2-litre engine. This was a development of the BMW engine brought back from Germany by H.J. Aldington as war reparation. Much of the car inherited BMW technology and proved popular both at home and abroad. When Norman Culpan's car finished third at Le Mans in 1949 the model was renamed Le Mans Replica. In 1951 Franco Cortese became the only driver to win the Targa Florio in a British car and there were numerous other successes for drivers such as Stirling Moss, Bob Gerard, Ken Wharton and Tony Crook, later owner of the Bristol Car Company. In 1952 a lighter and simpler chassis was used for the 'Mk II' model and the works car was raced with success by Ken Wharton and, later, Tony Brooks. A single-seater version was also developed for Formula 2 racing, though this suffered a weight disadvantage compared with the Cooper T20, which used the same power plant. There were other sports models from Frazer Nash, the 'Mille Miglia', 'Targa Florio', 'Sebring' and 'Le Mans Coupé' all having enveloping bodywork and all enjoying some competition experience. The Le Mans Replica formed the popular backbone of 2-litre sports car racing well into the 1950s. Including the original 'High Speed' model and the single-seaters, a total of 37 cars were built.

Actually a picture of the earlier Mk 1 model but illustrating well the stance of the car, this is Sid Greene's Frazer Nash Le Mans Replica driven in the 1952 Nine Hours by Tony Crook and Dick Jacobs.

Mike Hawthorn made a sensational debut in his Cooper Bristol T20. *(14/4/52 Photo: LAT Photographic)*

Another early Cooper, this time MG-engined, is driven early in an illustrious career by Jack Sears. *(17/5/52)*

The Nine Hours line-up includes the Falkner/Clarke Aston Martin DB2, the Baird/Salvadori Ferrari 225, the Whitehead/Cole Ferrari 225 and the Gerard/Clarke Frazer Nash. *(16/8/52)*

Winner of the Nine Hours Race was the Aston Martin DB3 of Peter Collins and Pat Griffith. *(16/8/52 Photo: LAT Photographic)*

Dr Giuseppe Farina waits on the grid for the start of the Woodcote Cup race. In the raincoat is the formidable Tony Vandervell, owner of the Ferrari Thinwall Special and father of the Vanwall. (27/9/52)

Scuderia Ambrosiana's Ferrari 125, driven by Bill Dobson in the F2 Madgwick Cup race. (27/9/52)

Stirling Moss, awaiting the start of the *Daily Graphic* Trophy in the cockpit of the G-type ERA, gazes thoughtfully at Louis Rosier's Ferrari 375/5. 'Perhaps if I had one of those... ?' *(27/9/52)*

Not even Stirling Moss could persuade the last ERA, the G-type, to be a winner. It was later passed to Bristol, who recreated the G-type as a team of sports cars with an enviable record at Le Mans. *(27/9/52)*

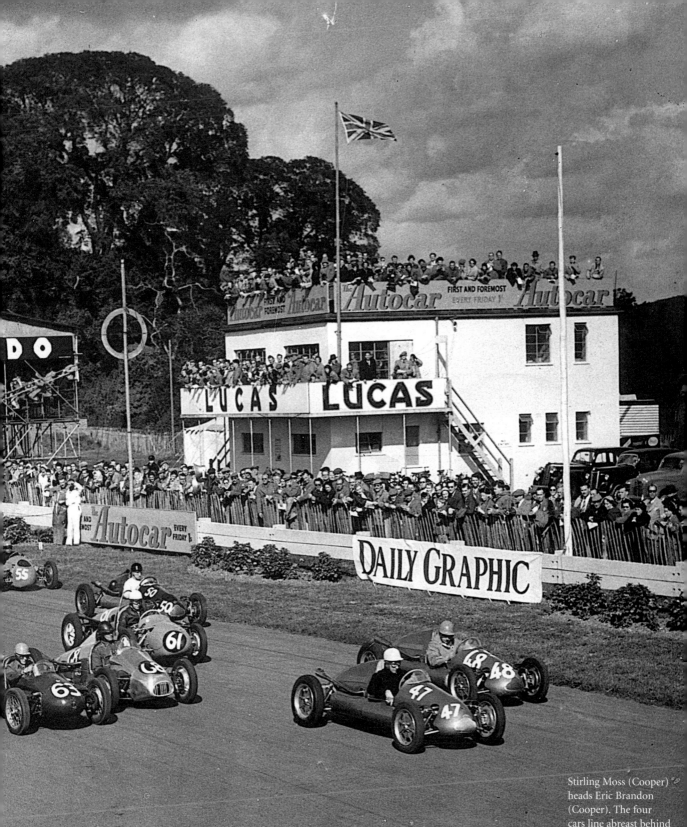

Stirling Moss (Cooper) heads Eric Brandon (Cooper). The four cars line abreast behind these two are (*left to right*) Don Parker (Kieft), Alan Brown (Cooper), Les Leston (Leston Special) and Reg Bicknell (Revis). (*27/9/52 Author's collection*)

The BRMs of Gonzalez (*left*) and Wharton sandwich Alan Brown's Cooper Bristol T20 at the start of the *Daily Graphic* Trophy race. Gonzalez led a BRM 1-2. *(27/9/52)*

The Maserati 8CM 3011 started a long career in the hands of Whitney Straight, who gave it the heart-shaped radiator. It was driven by Goodwood 'originator' Tony Gaze. *(27/9/52)*

Paul Emery (1916–1992)

In his early years Paul Emery worked with both his father George and Geoffrey Taylor of Alta Cars. The first Emery[and]son car appeared just after the war and was followed by a Lagonda Rapier-engined device driven by Eric Winterbottom. The engine was eventually replaced by the motor from the ex-Whitney Straight Duesenberg with the help of funds from Bobbie Baird. Emery moved on to a front-engined, front-wheel drive, rubber-suspended F3 car. Several cars were built (and sold) but Emery now turned to F2 with a larger version of the F3 chassis and an old Aston Martin engine. This proved too slow and was replaced by an Alta unit, later bored out to 2½ litres for F1 use. With this machine Emery was seen regularly in UK events though rarely finishing high up the order. A 2.4 Jaguar engine was tried before the car was sold in 1957. There were numerous other projects including the unraced C-type Connaught, bought at the closing-down auction and prepared for Bob Said to make an unsuccessful attempt at Indianapolis qualifying in 1959. Alan Brown backed Emery to move into the old Connaught works at Send to build rear-engined FJ and F1 cars in 1960. F1 cars were bought by Equipe National Belge but the car was never a success either in F1 or FJ guise. Hugh Powell bought into the team to support Tony Settember and eventually took over, renaming the operation Scirocco-Powell but, though improved, the cars were never winners. Emery moved on to numerous other ingenious projects and finally found fulfilment building and competing in midget racers for oval stadium racing. He was British champion for five years running. An inventive engineer who never had the resources to develop his designs, he was perhaps the last of the traditional British builders of specials.

Paul Emery in one of the few front-engined 500cc F3 cars to find even modest success, 27 May 1950.

1953

KING HUSSEIN of Jordan graced the first Member's Meeting of 1953 with his presence. The Aston Martin DB2 which he had entered non-started, but he toured the circuit in a vast open Lincoln.

Baron de Graffenried returned for the Easter meeting with the latest Formula 2 Maserati A6GCM. He was led by Salvadori's works fuel-injected Connaught, until he squeezed past on the final lap. Stirling Moss was still searching for a British car to match his talent. A team led by John Cooper of *The Autocar* magazine (not John Cooper of Cooper Cars) had put together an Alta-engined special on a Cooper chassis, but it was never a success and Moss could not get higher than seventh. A new Cooper Bristol, the T23, had been developed, and two were sold to Bob Gerard and Ken Wharton. An Alta-engined version (T24) was also built, one going to Peter Whitehead. A less likely variant was the Alfa Romeo-engined car of Bernie Rodger.

The 500cc race fell to Alan Brown's Francis Beart-tuned Cooper Norton, while the first handicap was won by Joe Goodhew's historic Darracq T150C. There were two BRMs in the Chichester Cup Libre race, driven by Parnell and Wharton. Mr Vandervell had engaged Italian Piero Taruffi to drive his Thin Wall. Ron Flockhart had obtained the unique ERA R4D from its only previous owner, Raymond Mays. The wet track suited the Swiss count in his Maserati, and he beat Wharton's BRM into second position while Parnell's BRM faltered and let Flockhart into third place. De Graffenried also won the second handicap race. The third handicap fell to the Ecurie Ecosse Cooper Bristol with Jimmy Stewart at the wheel. Though nowadays usually referred to as Jackie's older brother, Jimmy was actually a very fine driver in his own right and was a consistent Goodwood performer. The last handicap race went to larger-than-life car dealer Cliff Davis in the Tojeiro Bristol, which was subsequently cloned into the AC Ace.

Parnell's BRM again misbehaved in the 15-lap Richmond Trophy, leaving team-mate Wharton to win from Taruffi in the Thin Wall with de Graffenried third. The fuel-injected Connaught failed on the starting line, whereupon McAlpine hopped out of his car and handed it to Salvadori, who rewarded him with fourth place.

The BARC was to organise racing at the first meeting of the newly opened Crystal Palace circuit on Whit Monday, so the corresponding Goodwood date was dropped. This meant that the next major meeting at the Sussex circuit was the second running of the Nine Hours Race. The main protagonists were once again the works Aston Martin and Jaguar teams. The Aston drivers were paired Reg Parnell/Eric Thompson, Roy Salvadori/Dennis Poore and Peter Collins/Pat Griffith, while Jaguar had Stirling Moss/Peter Walker, Tony Rolt/Duncan Hamilton and Peter Whitehead/Ian Stewart. There were two more C-type Jaguars from Ecurie Ecosse for Jimmy Stewart/Bob Dickson and Jock Lawrence/Frank Curtis. The event was split into two classes rather than three, and it was in the smaller up to 2-litre class that the sole foreign entries were found, the works Gordini of Harry Schell and Jean Lucas and the Porsche 356 of Willi Buschmann and P.W.S. Pope. They were opposed by a gaggle of Frazer Nash with a mixture of Coopers, the Cliff Davis Tojeiro and single examples of Lester, Kieft and the Dargue MG Special.

In the larger class there were private Aston Martins, a works Austin Healey 100, two Allards and the HWM Jaguar of George Abecassis and Graham Whitehead, which proved fastest in practice. With the decline of HWM fortunes in Formula 2, Abecassis and Heath had put an XK engine into an early Formula 2 chassis and clothed it with a body originally intended for use on an Alta chassis. The Jaguar C (and later D)-type had been designed specifically with demands of Le Mans in mind. The HWM Jaguars were often to prove more nimble at Goodwood.

Aston Martin now had the DB3S with a 3-litre engine, and were determined to repeat their earlier success. Jaguar were fresh from victory at Le Mans but were headed in practice by the HWM and two of the Astons. Unusually, Moss was beaten in the sprint across the track by Harry Schell, but the Gordini refused to fire up and Moss led away. Salvadori stopped early with steering trouble and finally retired. Moss seemed to be acting as the hare to the Aston hounds. The Gordini had problems and Alan Brown's Cooper Bristol led the 2-litre class. This was the ex-Hawthorn Formula 2 car, rebodied as a two-seater.

Behind Brown was Cliff Davis, who drove the best part of a lap with the back of the Tojeiro ablaze, pausing briefly at the pits for it to be extinguished. Tony Rolt passed Moss who dropped back. Refuelling and driver changes saw the Moss/Walker car back in front, followed by Rolt/Hamilton, Whitehead/Stewart and Parnell/Thompson in the first Aston Martin. The leading car collided with the Porsche at Lavant Corner and Walker called at the pits to have the nose straightened. Moss took over a reduced lead. The Whitehead/Stewart car was passed by both Parnell and Griffith while pitting but Parnell had a tyre explode and lost fourth place as a result.

With the coming of darkness, Griffith lost some six minutes and third place in the pits with lighting and braking problems. An hour to go and Jaguar were ahead with Walker and Hamilton, but the second car appeared at the pits with low oil pressure and was immediately followed by Walker, coasting in with a thrown rod. Hamilton was sent on his way but returned a lap later with no oil pressure. Jaguars had led the entire race but now Eric Thompson was ahead and the Aston Martin pit speeded up Griffith in the third-placed car. Then the third works Jaguar slowed with a lack of brakes and oil pressure and Griffith was second. Aston Martin were again victorious and the Bob Gerard/David Clarke Frazer Nash won the 2-litre class, Frazer Nash taking the team prize.

The September meeting saw the debut of Sid Greene's Maserati A6GCS 2-litre sports car for Roy Salvadori to drive. He could only manage sixth in the sports car race won by George Abecassis in the HWM Jaguar, but made up for it with a Formula 2 win in the Connaught AL9. Stirling Moss finished second in the Cooper Alta, which had been put together in 11 days to replace the earlier car, which had been such a disappointment. Third was Tony Rolt in the Connaught owned by arch-enthusiast Rob Walker.

Mike Hawthorn was now a works Ferrari driver whose reputation had been made in the French Grand Prix, in which he beat Fangio in a wheel-to-wheel tussle. Mr Vandervell had obtained his services to pilot the Thin Wall, while Fangio himself appeared at the wheel of one of two BRMs, the other driven by Ken Wharton. Hawthorn left everyone else well behind, breaking the lap record in the process at 93.91mph. In 1958 Hawthorn said 'The 4½ litre Thin Wall Special is still today potentially the fastest car for the Goodwood circuit: a beautiful car to drive'. Salvadori was second behind Hawthorn in the Connaught until an oil pipe broke. The BRMs finished second and third with Moss fourth.

Don Parker won the 500cc race in his Kieft, from young Stuart Lewis-Evans in Francis Beart's Cooper. The handicap races fell to Peter Woozley's Allard and Graham Whitehead's ERA.

The Goodwood Trophy over 15 laps for Libre cars gave Hawthorn another victory and a chance to increase the lap record to 94.53mph. Fangio retired with gearbox problems, but Wharton brought the other BRM home second with Bob Gerard's Cooper Bristol third.

Adam Currie's early Lotus IIIb converted itself to a tricycle one chilly March day. (21/3/53)

Scarfe's very early Buckler scuttles through the chicane. Even a chilly March day did not deter a good-sized crowd. (21/3/53)

Stirling Moss in his bespoke Cooper Alta Special, which failed to perform and was replaced by a proprietary Cooper built up in 11 days by Alf Francis. *(6/4/53)*

The second generation Cooper Bristol T23 of Ken Wharton immaculate in green and yellow. Later its exhaust was re-routed to sweep down. Behind is Bill Aston's Aston Butterworth. *(6/4/53)*

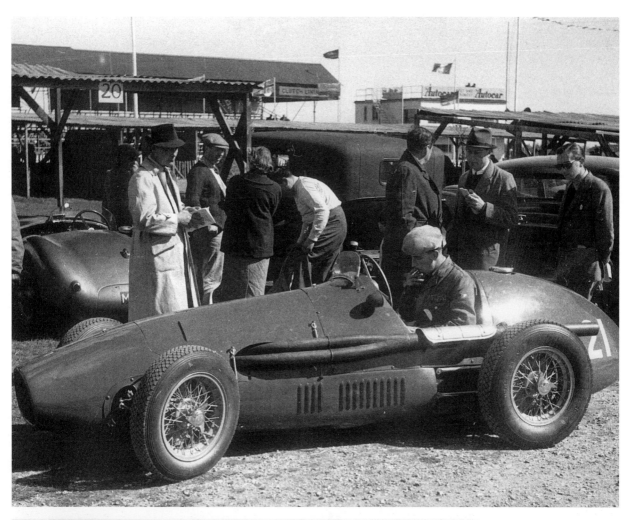

Bobby Baird waits behind the pits in his Ferrari 500 188/F2, ninth in the Lavant Cup for F2 cars.
(6/4/53)

Swiss aristocrat Baron Emanuel de Graffenried in his Maserati A6GCM 2038, winner of the F2 Lavant Cup race.
(6/4/53)

Harry Lester's MG-engined Lester coupe leads Robbie Mackenzie-Low's Jowett Jupiter through the chicane. *(2/5/53)*

Connaught's Lea Francis-engined sports car, driven by A.M. Goldthorpe. *(2/5/53)*

The Lotus VI was the first 'series production' sports car from Colin Chapman. Here Denis Wilkins drives chassis number 3. *(25/7/53)*

The rebodied Aston Martin DB3/7 of Tim Mayer and Philip Fotheringham-Parker, not as handsome as later Aston Martin coupes. *(22/8/53)*

The new Maserati A6GCS 2052 entered by Sid Greene's Gilby Engineering for Roy Salvadori. The hand-painted XMC601 may have been done in a hurry as the registration number subsequently appears as XEV601. *(26/9/53)*

Start of the Woodcote Cup with Mike Hawthorn in the Thinwall ahead of the BRMs of Juan Fangio (1) and Ken Wharton (2), the Connaughts of Roy Salvadori (10), Tony Rolt (11), Guy Jason-Henry (14) and Leslie Marr (12), Stirling Moss's '11-day wonder' Cooper Alta (7), Geoff Richardson's RRA (20), Jack Fairman's Turner (26) and Jock Somervail's ERA (19). *(26/9/53)*

Aston Martin DB3S

Aston Martin's DB3 model suffered from being a little tubby and overweight for its 3-litre engine. This unit had been stretched to its limit having started life at 2.3 litres, and the answer was found in the lighter chassis and more aerodynamic shape of the DB3S, which first appeared at Le Mans in 1953. The race saw all three works cars retire but the team had better luck for the remainder of the season, victory in the Goodwood Nine Hours and the Dundrod Tourist Trophy being the highlights.

1954 was a difficult year. Scarce resources were spent on the Lagonda V12 car which was never a success and the DB3S Coupés, built for Le Mans, were a disaster, both cars crashing. 1955 saw the introduction of disc brakes but Mercedes-Benz dominated the international scene. A second at Le Mans in 1956 alongside its new replacement, the DBR1, was the final international success of the DB3S. The works had built 10 cars for the team's use and another 21 for sale to customers, the car racing all over the world. The DBR1 was to bring the team the success that it had worked so hard to achieve.

Aston Martin DB3S/4 came second in the 1953 Nine Hours, driven by Peter Collins and Pat Griffith.

Ken Wharton (1916–1957)

A true all-rounder, Ken Wharton was a success at trials, rallies and races. The Smethwick garage proprietor began competing before World War Two. He won the RAC Trials Championship in successive years and took three Tulip Rallies. He was Hill Climb Champion four years in a row. On the tracks he raced an F2 Frazer Nash followed by a new Cooper Bristol. He struggled with the V16 BRM and also drove the Maserati 250F, which the Owen Organisation bought to tide them over until their new Formula 1 car arrived. He drove the early Vanwall in 1955 and crashed badly at Silverstone. After an unproductive year in 1956 he was killed when his Ferrari Monza crashed in New Zealand.

Ken Wharton in his smart Cooper Bristol T23 at the 1953 Easter meeting.

1954

A NEW FORMULA 1 came into operation for 1954. A limit of 2½ litres allowed the older Formala 2 cars to compete but left the BRM and Thin Wall with nowhere to race but the odd Formule Libre race – which in reality was all they had had in the previous two years. It was strange timing that the Owen Organisation should choose this time to introduce a Mk 2 version of the V16, lightened and with a shorter wheelbase, when opportunities to exercise the beast were diminishing.

It was perhaps a little ambitious to open the Easter meeting with a seven-lap race for the new Grand Prix formula cars, but there were four in attendance. HWM had stretched the Alta engine to 2½ litres, as had Peter Whitehead (Cooper Alta). The ex-Baird F2 Ferrari 500 had gone back to the factory for a 2½-litre engine and was now run by Scuderia Ambrosiana for Reg Parnell. There was one brand-new proper Grand Prix car present – Sid Greene's Maserati 250F for Roy Salvadori. Formula 2 cars made up the remaining entry but Reg Parnell won from Salvadori with Ken McAlpine's Connaught third.

BRM brought two cars for the Chichester Cup five-lap Formule Libre race, one each of the Mk 1 and Mk 2, for Ken Wharton and Ron Flockhart. The Formula 1/Formula 2 field was also joined by Jock Somervail's ERA R12B, though the Thin Wall was missing, as were its intended driver Alberto Ascari, and de Graffenried's Maserati. Wharton won in the new-style BRM but was harried all the way by Roy Salvadori's Maserati 250F. New boy Flockhart, starting from second on the grid, got elbowed off in the crush of the first corner and restarted in last place. He drove through the field to good effect, finishing fourth behind Reg Parnell's Ferrari.

Les Leston won the Formula 3 race in the works Cooper Norton, while the handicaps went to Jimmy Stewart, Tony Crook, Tony Rolt and Claude Hamilton.

The principal race was again for Formule Libre cars and saw a repeat of the Wharton/Salvadori duel with the BRM driver this time in the older car. The race was over 21 laps, or just over 50 miles, and Flockhart was leading in the newer BRM until the experimental magneto let him down. Wharton inherited the lead with Salvadori on his tail, though Parnell dropped out with gearbox bothers. Repeatedly Salvadori attempted to pass the BRM. Though he could draw alongside there was never quite enough power on tap to get past. On lap 19 the BRM slid sideways and was charged amidships by the Maserati. Salvadori spun off and stalled while Wharton kept going to the finish. The mechanics examined the BRM and decided it was irreparable and so the Mk 1 ended its career. From failing to leave the start line in its first race to winning its last with a written-off car and through many extraordinary adventures along the way, this had been one remarkable, though unsuccessful, racing car.

Salvadori's team lodged a protest – a rare event in the 1950s – but the stewards decided that the BRM win would stand. Almost unnoticed, Kenneth McAlpine was second and Leslie Marr third, both in Connaughts. Salvadori later recounted: 'I received from the Duke of Richmond and Gordon a silver cigarette box inscribed "In acknowledgement of a splendid show at Goodwood on Easter Monday 19th April 1954". I was quite convinced that the Duke thought I had been hard done by until I learned that Ken Wharton had also been presented with a similar cigarette box'.

The Members' Meeting on 1 May was remarkable for the presence of the Ecurie Ecosse team, with drivers Jimmy Stewart and Ninian Sanderson in their C-type Jaguars. Three more C-types were driven by Duncan Hamilton, Hans Davids and John Keeling, but it was Jimmy Stewart who won both scratch races for the bigger sports cars. The race for cars up to 1½ litres included Frank Nichols in the CSM, a car he helped to create before the Elva marque was born.

The Whitsun meeting was back on the calendar for 1954. It was curious that the first race, for Formula 3 cars and poorly supported, was over 15 laps, while the second, for Formula 1 cars, was over a mere five laps. Reg Bicknell won the former in his Revis Norton, while Reg Parnell's Ferrari won the Formula 1 race. Roy Salvadori's Maserati 250F hesitated on the start line while its driver searched for a suitable gear. When eventually under way, Salvadori scythed through the field in a superb demonstration of both the driver's skill and the car's potential.

For the first time the main race for the Johnson's Challenge Trophy featured sports cars. Ecurie Ecosse brought three C-type Jaguars for Jimmy Stewart, Ninian Sanderson and Sir James Scott Douglas. Other C-types were driven by Gerry Dunham, John Keeling, Berwyn Baxter and Michael Head. Salvadori was in the Gilby Engineering Maserati A6GCS and Colin Chapman had the streamlined Lotus Mk VIII with MG power. The Scottish cars were surprisingly far down the line at the Le Mans start, in 12th, 13th and 14th positions, but it was Stewart and Sanderson making the running with Dunham in third place. Salvadori pulled the Maserati into fourth place to take the 2-litre class and Chapman won the 1½-litre section.

The Whitsun Trophy for Formule Libre cars featured two of the latest 'Mk II' BRMs for Ken Wharton and Ron Flockhart. Tony Vandervell had obtained the services of one of Britain's fastest rising stars, Peter Collins, to drive his Ferrari Thin Wall Special. Salvadori and Parnell provided the most serious opposition, mixed in with the usual F2 runners and a couple of ERAs. Paul Emery had produced an interesting series of one-off single-seaters and his latest very neat creation with Alta power was driven by Colin Chapman. The creator of Lotus cars was a fine racing driver and it is surprising to realise that his handful of races in the Emeryson represent his only single-seater drives. He did practice a Vanwall for the French Grand Prix of 1956, but he crashed and missed the race. Even more surprising is that he never started a race in a Lotus single-seater. Flockhart led the race initially but Collins pushed him hard and took the lead on lap five. Salvadori passed Wharton into third place and Parnell came home fifth. Chapman finished last but one.

The two handicap races were won by the Aston Martin DB3 of Sir Jeremy Boles (entrant to a most promising young driver, Don Beauman) and the Triumph TR2 of Irishman Desmond Titterington, who would make his name as a member of Ecurie Ecosse.

A great success at the Members' Meetings in 1954 was the RWG of Roy Watling-Greenwood. This very neat special, with MG suspension and Ford Ten engine, won the *Motor Sport* Brooklands Memorial Trophy by a single point from John Coombs's Lotus. Also enjoying success was Tony Brooks in Hely's Frazer Nash Le Mans Replica. Another name to appear in the entry lists in 1954 was Innes Ireland.

Due to the effort and cost involved there was no Nine Hours Race in 1954, but the quality of the entry for the September meeting went some way to make up for this disappointment. The Madgwick Cup F2 race found six A-type Connaught Altas up against six Cooper Bristols, one Cooper Alta, Horace Richard's trusty HAR and John Webb's Turner (which non-started). Bob Gerard showed that he had lost none of his skill in winning from Don Beauman's Connaught and Mike Keen's Cooper Alta.

The entry for the F3 event was so large that it was split into two races. The 'senior' race went to Don Parker's Kieft over Stirling Moss's Beart Cooper, with Reg Bicknell's Revis Norton third.

The whole season had seen a continual struggle for the 2-litre sports car class between the Gilby Maserati A6GCS of Roy Salvadori and a new marque, the Lister Bristol, driven by Archie Scott Brown. Archie has become a motor-racing legend, not only as a result of his successes but because he achieved this despite a malformed right hand and legs that were distorted and short. He faced opposition to his racing in the early days of his career but this was overcome by the sheer ability that he demonstrated. At least, it was overcome in the UK. Overseas he was to face frequent rejection on medical grounds and earlier in 1954 he had had his competition licence withdrawn by the RAC. Though it had been returned by the time of the September meeting at Goodwood, there was some doubt about whether the BARC would accept his entry. Brian Lister therefore arranged a replacement driver – Stirling Moss. It quietly amused Archie that Moss was beaten (albeit by the narrowest of margins) by Salvadori. Archie himself had beaten Salvadori so the Scott Brown reputation was done no harm.

In truth the race had been remarkably close, with the Lister and Maserati often side by side. Behind this pair came Alan Brown in the converted ex-Hawthorn Cooper Bristol, Tony Crook in another Cooper converted to sports configuration and Tony Brooks in Hely's Frazer Nash. These three were engaged in a struggle just as fierce as that of the leaders and were separated by about three seconds at the finish. Bringing up the rear were three Triumph TR2s. After five laps they finished about two minutes behind the leaders, and the leader of the three was an American with the glorious name of James E. Pennybacker.

For the 21-lap Goodwood Trophy F1 race, the F2 entry was supplemented by the Salvadori Maserati 250F and Reg Parnell's Ferrari 500/625. This was to be the first Goodwood appearance of the Maserati 250F bought by Stirling Moss. However, Moss had now been co-opted into the works Maserati team as a result of his gallant efforts over a season that had included a heart-breaking Italian Grand Prix, which saw retirement from the lead. The greatest benefit of works backing was someone else to underwrite the cost of repairs and the consequent ability to push the car to its limits. Yet another 250F was handled by French veteran Louis Rosier, though the similar car that the BRM team had bought to keep their hand in was to be a non-starter. BRMs eternal rival Tony Vandervell was ahead of them with the development of his own F1 car. Originally intended for F2, the Vanwall Special featured an engine owing much to Norton motorcycles (Vandervell was a director of Nortons) and a chassis built by Coopers. Ted Whiteaway's HWM and Paul Emery's Emeryson both had engines stretched to 2½ litres. Moss was unbeatable but Peter Collins brought the new Vanwall home second with Salvadori third.

The unlimited sports car race also had a quality entry. Roy Salvadori and Desmond Titterington drove Ecurie Ecosse C-type Jaguars, Cliff Davis taking over the Gilby Maserati A6GCS with a view to the possibility of buying the car for 1955. There were two HWM Jaguars for George Abecassis and Jack Fairman and a Ferrari 750 Monza for Mike Hawthorn. The car belonged to Irishman Joe Kelly, who probably had an arrangement with Ferrari to allow Hawthorn to drive the car on suitable occasions. Another Ferrari was the 4½-litre 375MM Spider brought across the Atlantic by young Masten Gregory. Graham Whitehead had one of the first Aston Martin DB3Ss in private hands, but it was Salvadori who made the running with Gregory storming along in his wake. The big Ferrari was a bit of a handful and Gregory had to give way to Hawthorn until the smaller Ferrari broke its differential. Gregory could not get on terms with Salvadori who won by the smallest of margins with Abecassis third.

The Woodcote Cup Formule Libre race was another opportunity to give the two short chassis BRMs and the Thin Wall an outing. Ken Wharton and Ron Flockhart were to drive the BRMs and Mike Hawthorn was entered in the Thin Wall. However, he switched to the Vanwall, perhaps to experience this new F1 car in comparison to his usual Ferrari. This left the Thin Wall to Peter Collins, but it was Wharton who took an early lead. Collins was soon on his heels and, as the BRM seemed to go off tune, he rushed by and pulled out a six-second lead. Wharton hung on to second place ahead of Moss and Hawthorn. Meanwhile Flockhart ran out of road and deranged the front suspension of the second BRM. The Vanwall put in an impressive performance. Best of the F2 brigade was Bob Gerard in his Cooper Bristol.

The meeting and the season closed with the 'junior' F3 race, won by Noel Berrow Johnson in his Martin Norton ahead of a gaggle of Coopers.

1954
Maserati 250F

Many people's favourite F1 car of all time, the 250F Maserati was introduced for the 1954 2½-litre formula. Had it not been for the Mercedes-Benz domination of the 1954 and 1955 seasons, the 250F would probably have had an even more successful career, but it did manage to race in the first and last Grands Prix run to that formula. Popular with drivers for its friendly handling, the car provided the backbone to the formula. Some 26 cars were produced either for the factory team or the numerous private entrants who were able to take part in F1 racing in those very different times. Its straight-six engine was developed from the previous F2 and produced a claimed 240bhp in 1954. Four cars came to the UK, 2504 for 'B Bira',

2507 for Gilby Engineering (Roy Salvadori), 2508 for Stirling Moss and 2509 for the BRM team. Stirling Moss's F1 career was finally launched by this car. He was soon adopted into the Maserati works team and 1955 saw him alongside Fangio at Mercedes. Between 1954 and 1958 there were few F1 races across Europe in which a 250F did not feature in the top six. The cars were developed over this period, a lightweight chassis being brought in for the works cars in 1957. Fangio won his fifth and final world championship in these cars. Though they tried a V12 engine and also the ultra-lightened 'Piccolo' model, the end of the line came in 1958. There comes a time when a second-hand racing car changes from being an outdated piece of kit into being a highly desirable historic machine, and Goodwood was to see the Maserati 250F achieve this transition. It was just as delightful the second time round.

Stirling Moss in his Maserati 250F 2508, winner of the Goodwood Trophy race on 25 September 1954.

Elva creator Frank Nichols, seen here in a Lotus VI ahead of M.C. Litton's MG at the opening 1954 Members' Meeting. *(27/3/54)*

Gerry Ruddock's Lester MG sports a 'streamlined' front end. He registered fourth place in his scratch race and fifth in his handicap race. *(27/3/54)*

The Hon. Edward
Greenall negotiates the
the chicane in his very
smart Cooper Norton,
tenth in the Earl of
March Trophy.
(19/4/54)

Tony Crook's re-
bodied Cooper Alta
T24 winning the
Second Easter
Handicap. Fitted with a
Bristol engine this one
and a half seater was
very successful.
(19/4/54)

Not seen so often, the
ERAs were still racing
in 1954. Here Claude
Hamilton drives R1B
to victory in the Fourth
Easter Handicap.
(19/4/54)

Keith Hall drives
Border Reivers' Cooper
Norton to ninth place
in the Earl of March
Trophy F3 race.
(19/4/54)

Cooper chassis but with Alta rather than Bristol power for Peter Whitehead. The car was subsequently bought by Jack Brabham on his arrival in England. *(19/4/54)*

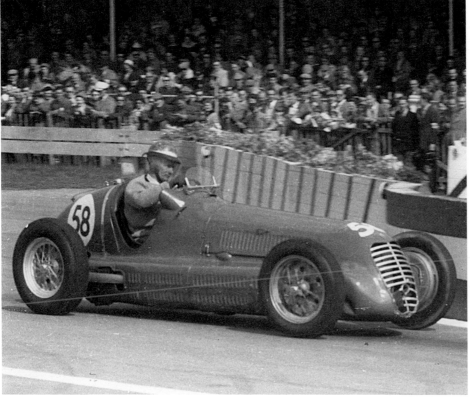

Preserver of several historic cars, Joe Goodhew gives his Maserati 4CL some exercise late in its long life. *(19/4/54)*

Bob Berry, Jaguar development engineer, in his lightweight XK120 capable of mixing it with the C-types. *(1/5/54)*

Entered by Vermin Stables, Jocelyn Stevens finished tenth in his scratch race in the Aston Martin DB3/10. *(1/5/54)*

Allards pioneered the large American-engined sports car concept in the UK. Here is Robin Carnegie's J2. *(1/5/54)*

Bob Walshaw's Lotus Ford Mk VI was rather out of its depth against the more specialised sports-racing machines. *(7/6/54)*

Start of the 1250cc scratch race with Michael MacDowel's Lotus VI (4), Frank Nichols's CSM (6), Richard Manwaring's Lotus VI (1), Mitchell's MG (9), Edward Lewis's Lotus VI (5), E.H. Heath's MG Special (8), Bryan Hewitt's MG TD (11), Roy Watling-Greenwood's RWG (7), F.L. Rowke's MG TF (10), Martin Gadsby's Riley (3) and Dickie Metcalfe's Fiat Balilla (14). (21/8/54)

This Emeryson Jaguar
driven by Bob Dennis
is actually Aston
Martin DB3/6 fitted
with a Jaguar C-type
engine and Emery
body modifications
including the hard top
used by the works at Le
Mans 1952. *(21/8/54)*

Tom Dargue's MG
Special comes into
contact with Harry
Digby's Lotus VI/38.
Both retired from the
1500cc Scratch Race on
the penultimate lap.
(21/8/54)

Ecurie Richmond's
Cooper Norton driven
by Eric Brandon, sixth
in the senior 500cc
race. *(25/9/54)*

Bob Gerard's Cooper
Bristol T23 clears the
chicane on his way to
victory in the
Madgwick Cup F2
race. *(25/9/54)*

Stirling Moss in Francis
Beart's Cooper Norton,
chased by Reg
Bicknell's Revis Norton
with its individual
streamlined nose.
(25/9/54)

Young American
Masten Gregory,
undaunted by the
mighty 4.5-litre Ferrari
375MM Spider,
finished second in the
unlimited sports car
race. *(25/9/54)*

Mike Hawthorn drives
Joe Kelly's Ferrari 750
Monza to retirement in
the unlimited sports
car race. *(25/9/54)*

Tony Vandervell's new
Vanwall Special driven
by Mike Hawthorn in
the Woodcote Cup
Formule Libre race.

Roy Salvadori (1922–)

Successor to Reg Parnell as 'King of Goodwood', Roy Salvadori was born in Essex to Italian parents. Surviving a particularly nasty accident at Silverstone early in his racing career, he continued to drive a huge variety of cars on circuits all over the world. He may not have experienced the international success of his contemporaries Moss, Hawthorn, Collins and Brooks, but he probably put in more racing miles and scored more than his fair share of wins. After a year with Connaught in 1953 he drove the Gilby Engineering Maseratis with great success and followed this with works Grand Prix drives with Cooper, BRM and Aston Martin. He was a member of the Aston Martin sports car team from 1953 until they finished racing. The high point must have been his Le Mans victory with Carroll Shelby in 1959. Reg Parnell employed him in 1961 in the Yeoman Credit F1 team but the Coopers they used were not a match for Ferrari and Lotus. They had high hopes of Lola in the following year but teammate Surtees had the best of the results and Salvadori decided to give up single-seaters while continuing with sports and saloons. Tommy Atkins and John Coombs provided him with the best machinery and he continued his winning ways until 1965 when he finally retired. He moved back to Coopers, this time as team manager, before final retirement in the late 1960s. His presence at modern-day historic gatherings brings back a flood of happy memories to all who saw his skill behind the wheel of such a variety of cars.

Roy Salvadori contemplates his prospects in the Gilby Maserati 250F.

1955

T HE BARC agreed to organise the British Grand Prix for 1955, not at
Goodwood, but at the recently opened circuit beside the Grand
National course at Aintree. Following his successful year with the
Maserati, Stirling Moss had been rewarded with a works drive alongside
Fangio at Mercedes Benz. Mike Hawthorn, on the other hand, had forsaken
Ferrari for a seat in Tony Vandervell's Vanwall (the word 'Special' having been
dropped from its title).

The Vanwall was not ready in time for the Easter meeting and Mercedes
were not in the habit of attending such non-championship events. Stirling
Moss entered his own Maserati 250F, which legendary mechanic Alf Francis
had modified with Dunlop disc brakes, wheels and tyres and SU fuel injection.
Mike Hawthorn was able to take the weekend off. Tony Rolt drove the new
GP Connaught on its first appearance. The 'B-type' was clothed in a handsome
all-enveloping body, which may or may not have been of aerodynamic
advantage, but was certainly a handful when dismantled in the pits and
decidedly prone to damage.

The meeting began with the F2 Lavant Cup, the usual assortment of
Coopers and Connaughts added to by Emeryson, Turner and HAR plus Mike
Anthony's sports Lotus Bristol Mk X. Roy Salvadori was back at the wheel of
a Connaught. The car, owned by John Young, was the last A-series car to be
built and one of two with a 7ft 6in wheelbase. Bob Gerard's Cooper Bristol led
for the first five laps but Salvadori found a way past on the penultimate lap. In
third place came Don Beauman in Sir Jeremy Boles's Connaught, ahead of
Mike Keen's Cooper Alta.

Coopers had again been busy. The Coventry Climax engine had made its
racing debut in 1954 and its potential was obvious. Coopers built a rear-
engined sports car with a central seat and chopped-off rear end, apparently of

aerodynamic significance but actually a necessity. It was otherwise too long for the transporter, or so the story goes. Others to use the engine included Eric Brandon in his self-built car known as the Halseylec, a second car appearing later in the season and, of course, Lotus who put it in Mks VI, VIII and IX, as it became more widely available. Kieft had been the first to use it but they were absent on the day.

Another chassis to carry the new engine was a combined effort of Bernie Rodger and Francis Beart and designated the Beart Rodger T66. The two men were friends of Stirling Moss who agreed to drive the untried little car. 1955 was the year in which Stirling Moss won the Tourist Trophy, the Targa Florio, the Mille Miglia and British Grand Prix. Few would argue that his skill was second only to the great Fangio, and yet here he was on bank holiday Monday driving an uncompetitive one-off car in order to help his friends.

Connaughts had used two spare A-type F2 chassis as the basis of a sports model, the AL/SR. The first was sold to John Coombs and then on to Peter Bell for Les Leston to drive. The second was kept by the works and rebodied in a similar style to the new B-type F1 car. Both had 1500cc engines, as did John Coombs's Lotus Mk VIII, which used the Connaught engine from the first AL/SR. Colin Chapman's Lotus Mk IX used the more traditional 1500cc MG engine, but the original Coventry Climax engines were of 1098cc, giving Ivor Bueb's new Cooper too much to do. The two Connaughts made the running with Leston passing McAlpine on the second lap and continuing to victory despite a paling protruding from the front wing after a brush with the chicane. Bueb managed to hold off Coombs for third place. The Climax engine performed well and the small-engined sports car was destined to become the entry-level category for some years to come.

Although just one ERA (Richard Cobden's R10B) and the famous ex-Straight/Bira Maserati 8CM turned up, the only justification for a Formule Libre race at an international meeting was as an excuse to run the V16 BRM again. With a 2½-litre F1 car in prospect, BRM had the services of Peter Collins as their number one driver. His season with the Thin Wall had certainly given him a feel for big powerful cars and he won the race from pole position. The Moss Maserati was not at its best as the increased power from the fuel injection had upset the road-holding. He could only manage third place behind Roy Salvadori's similar car, with Tony Rolt bringing the exotic new Connaught home fourth.

In eighth place came the ex-Peter Whitehead Cooper Alta, driven with a lot of sideways motion by an Australian in his European debut – Jack Brabham. Gregor Grant of *Autosport* wrote of Brabham: 'This Aussie is certainly a presser-onner and possesses remarkable control over his car. More will be heard of this young gentleman'.

The Earl of March Trophy race was a typical F3 thrash. The 500cc cars were quite closely matched and usually produced close and exciting racing. Ivor Bueb had the works Cooper Norton while Les Leston was in the Francis Beart-tuned car and the pair passed and re-passed throughout the race. Behind them Don Parker's Kieft fought with the Coopers of Eric Brandon, future F1 constructor Ken Tyrrell and Colin Davis, son of legendary artist, journalist and Bentley Boy, Sammy Davis. Leston finished a close second on the road but was penalised 15 seconds for a jumped start and was classified fifth.

The first D-type Jaguar in private hands went to Duncan Hamilton. This was the car with which he and Tony Rolt had finished second in the 1954 Le Mans. Ecurie Ecosse brought just one C-type down from Scotland for Tony Rolt to drive. Two private Ferrari 750 Monzas arrived for Mike Sparken and Luigi Piotti. The first Aston Martin DB3S was sold to Roy Salvadori and the second to Peter Collins. Hamilton and Sparken provided yet another tooth and nail conflict at the front. Salvadori was comfortably third while Rolt and Collins struggled over fourth place. However, both the leaders were penalised for jumping the start and Salvadori found himself the winner.

Coopers had built a front-engined car to enable Gilby Engineering to try their Maserati engine in a lighter set up. It was not a great success and Salvadori finished fourth in the 2-litre sports car race. The winner was Archie Scott Brown in the Lister Bristol, but by the narrowest of margins over Tony Brooks, now promoted to the works Frazer Nash Le Mans Replica. The two provided yet another ding-dong battle for the lead with Mike Anthony's Bristol engined Lotus Mk X in third spot.

The two Maseratis of Moss and Salvadori made the running in the Richmond Trophy F1 race, until, that is, Salvadori spun at the chicane and dropped back to sixth. He tigered back through the field to such good effect that he was in the lead by lap 12 when Moss retired with fuel bothers. Although the lead was no longer in dispute, the race lost none of its excitement as Gerard and Beauman disputed second place with Keen, Brabham and Rolt fighting behind them. Brabham ran out of fuel and Rolt retired but the scrapping throughout the field had kept the crowd entertained.

For its final Goodwood appearance the BRM, with Collins at the helm, started from scratch in the final handicap race. Five laps were insufficient to get him higher than fifth, but the car was on song and recorded the fastest lap by a BRM. Bob Gerard won the race from Salvadori. Salvadori summed up his performance thus: 'I won three races and was second in two. We earned near to £1,000 in starting money. Prize and bonus money increased this to around £2,000.'

The Whitsun meeting was again to feature sports cars with three ten-lap 'heats' and a 21-lap final. Mike Hawthorn flew back from the continent to drive a new Tojeiro Bristol, which sadly expired during his special Monday morning practice session.

The 1500cc race, which opened proceedings, demonstrated the strengthening popularity of this class. Besides the Lotus and Cooper regulars there were cars from Tojeiro, Lester, Arnott and Griffiths. The Beart Rodger driven by Moss at Easter had Jack Fairman at the wheel. Colin Chapman was the winner in his Lotus MG Mk IX, overtaking Reg Parnell's Cooper Connaught at the very last bend. Kenneth McAlpine's Connaught AL/SR was third.

Despite Hawthorn's absence from the 2-litre race, the entry was almost as large as the earlier event. Both Mike Anthony and Peter Scott Russell had Bristol-engined Lotus Mk Xs, and there were now Lister Bristols in private teams for David Hampshire and Allan Moore. Tony Brooks was the fastest of the three Frazer Nash LM Replicas and there were two of the new AC Aces, the quickest driven by Ken Rudd. The Triumph TR2s were somewhat overshadowed but the model would prove a practical car for many club drivers over future seasons. Anthony's Lotus Bristol was victorious and Scott Russell would have been second but his car went off song and had to give way to Tony Brooks.

A second D-type Jaguar joined Duncan Hamilton's original car in the over 2-litre heat. Entered by Jack Broadhead, it was driven by Jaguar development engineer Bob Berry, who had put up sterling performances in his XK120. They finished first and second with Dick Protheroe's older C-type keeping Peter Blond's similar car at bay. Next to finish was the HWM Jaguar, driven on this occasion by John Heath, its co-originator making one of his infrequent appearances behind the wheel. The Cooper family of cars had been expanded again to include a Jaguar-engined sports car, driven here by Cyril Wick. He was challenging for third place on the last lap when he lost control and charged the bank in spectacular style at Woodcote corner, happily without serious injury.

In a bid for variety, the following three races were something of a novelty. The handicap for vintage cars proved entertaining. Tozer's wonderful sounding Amilcar C6 beat Jack Sears's 1914 GP Sunbeam with Bentleys taking the next three places. Davenport's well known GN Spider was involved in an incongruous duel with Clutton's enormous 12-litre Itala.

Next came a race for the ladies, not at all politically correct by today's standards, won by Nancy Mitchell's stately Daimler Conquest. The handicappers gave Pat Moss just too much to overcome.

The handicap for 'celebrities' was won at a trot by Richard 'Stinker' Murdoch's Rolls Royce 20/25 at a speed of under 50mph. It was not a great spectacle and was not repeated.

The Johnsons Challenge Trophy featured the fastest from the three sports car races and provided another win for Duncan Hamilton with Bob Berry and Mike Anthony following.

The Members' Meetings were seeing large numbers of Lotus and Coopers, but there were still some older cars mixed in. Driving a Riley at the June meeting was Innes Ireland, who was to progress rapidly over the next two years.

What was to be the final Nine Hours Race took place on 20 August 1955. The paying public had not supported the event in sufficient numbers to make it a commercial success. Aston Martin were obviously intent on scoring their hat-trick. There were to be no works Jaguars, but four private D-types appeared. The motor racing world was still reeling from the shock of the Le Mans tragedy, which had killed over 80 spectators and the driver Pierre Levegh. Many races had been cancelled across Europe and motorsport had been banned in Switzerland, a restriction that applies to this day.

Other serious opposition to the Astons came from three Ferrari 750 Monzas, privately entered but with obvious works support even to the extent of a spare car for practice. It was an odd decision to provide these cars with side-lifting jacks rather than the more usual fore and aft arrangement. This meant that the cars had to be manoeuvred across the pit lane to change wheels, not an aid to quick pit stops and also blocking the road to the annoyance of other drivers.

There were old favourites in the Aston line up, with Reg Parnell paired with Roy Salvadori and Peter Walker with Dennis Poore, but Peter Collins had new boy Tony Brooks. The second production DB3S was to be shared by Australians Tony Gaze and David McKay. Duncan Hamilton entered two D-type Jaguars for himself and Tony Rolt, Peter Whitehead and Michael Head. Bob Berry shared Broadhead's car with Jaguar test driver Norman Dewis, and Ecurie Ecosse had one car for Desmond Titterington and Ninian Sanderson. HWM had two Jaguar-engined cars for Lance Macklin/Bill Smith and John Marshall/Dick Protheroe. An older Aston Martin DB3 and Bertie Bradnack's Cooper Jaguar completed the over 2-litre class.

The works Lister Bristol was shared by Allan Moore and Bill Holt, while John Green's car was driven by David Hampshire and Peter Scott Russell. Bob Chase had a Bristol engine insinuated into the rear of a Cooper 'Bobtail' for Mike Keen/Mike Anthony and Tony Crook shared his earlier car with Dick Gibson. Cliff Davis had sold his Tojeiro Bristol, which was to be driven by the Rolls brothers while he shared his Lotus Bristol Mk X with Reg Bicknell. Bert Rogers and Percy Crabb had a newer Tojeiro Bristol which was probably the car which Hawthorn tried at Whitsun. The final entry in the 2-litre class was the sole Frazer Nash, a Sebring model in the hands of Dickie Stoop and Peter Wilson.

The under 2-litre class found both Connaught AL/SRs for Kenneth McAlpine/Eric Thompson and Les Leston/Archie Scott Brown, although why Archie was not in the Lister is not clear. Porsche sent over a single 550 for Stirling Moss to drive with von Hanstein while Wolfgang Seidel shared his own car with Dick Steed. John Coombs/John Young had the former's Connaught-engined Lotus Mk IX, with works cars driven by Colin Chapman/Peter Jopp (MG engine) and Ron Flockhart/Cliff Allison (Climax engine). Paul Emery and Tony Page shared another MG-engined Mk IX. Coopers for Tommy Sopwith/Peter Blond, Jim Russell/Ivor Bueb and Roy Watling Green-wood/Dennis Barthel left only the streamlined HRG of David Calvert and Richard Green to complete the entry.

That Aston Martin were serious became clear when they installed a radio link with a 'spotter' at the chicane. As the cars passed the slowest point on the circuit, it was the spotter's job to check on tyre wear and keep the pits advised. Fastest in practice had been the Mike Hawthorn/de Portago Ferrari, Jean Jonneret/Ken Wharton managing sixth, with Harry Schell/Jean Lucas eighth despite the theoretical advantage of Messier disc brakes on the Schell car. The Astons filled second, third and fourth places on the Le Mans line up. Although Les Leston was the first under way, Hawthorn was in the lead by Madgwick corner. As the whole pack squirmed around the circuit, it was Tony Gaze who became the victim of the almost inevitable coming together as he spun his Aston Martin at St Mary's, knocking off the front suspension of Flockhart's Lotus as he did so. Aston Martin suffered a severe blow when Reg Parnell coasted in with hub failure. Rolt retired his Jaguar out in the country while Hawthorn held on to his lead from the two remaining Aston Martins until he rolled into the pits with no available gears. He rejoined the race seven laps behind Collins and Walker.

Further down the field, Bert Rogers had one or two lurid moments in the Tojeiro Bristol before inverting the car at Lavant Corner. He was able to drive back to the pits. Mike Keen was not so lucky when his Cooper somersaulted and caught fire. He later died of his injuries.

Though Harry Schell now had his Ferrari up to second place, Hawthorn's efforts to make up for lost time were set back by a pit stop of 3½ minutes to change just one wheel. Stirling Moss handed over the Porsche to von Hanstein, who proved to be about 10 seconds a lap slower. Colin Chapman was able to draw out a lead in the under 2-litre class, pursued by Archie Scott Brown's Connaught.

Dennis Poore lost the gear knob on his Aston Martin, the lever chewing his hand before both were wrapped in tape at his next pit stop. The Titterington/Sanderson Ecurie Ecosse Jaguar now held the lead from the Collins/Brooks Aston and the Macklin/Smith HWM. The next move was into the lead by Collins/Brooks. The Head/Whitehead Jaguar charged the bank at Woodcote and Titterington hit a row of markers, wiping out a headlight as darkness came, the resulting repair effectively costing the Scottish team the race. Chapman was put out by a detached flywheel and Schell went out when the gearbox cried enough.

Moss retook the lead in his class and the Cliff Davis/Reg Bicknell Lotus Bristol led the 2-litre class until they lost 25 minutes with a burned-out dynamo. The hard-used Hawthorn/de Portago Ferrari broke its back axle, leaving the Wharton/Jonneret car as the last Ferrari, some 17 laps adrift, but it too retired with a broken crankcase. Then Collins brought in the Aston Martin with ignition bothers and the Walker/Poore Aston took on the lead. Despite losing second gear, the DB3S managed to stay ahead of the Scottish Jaguar, which was catching it a the rate of eight seconds a lap.

So it was that Aston Martin won their hat-trick. The Collins/Brooks car came third behind the Titterington/Sanderson Jaguar. The David Hampshire/Peter Scott Russell Lister Bristol and the Les Leston/Archie Scott Brown Connaught took the class honours.

George Abecassis in his HWM Jaguar won the *Motor Sport* trophy. The Members' Meeting entry lists were now including many of the country's leading drivers, such as Colin Chapman, John Coombs, Duncan Hamilton and Graham Whitehead. The novices were still there but, with the new generation of specialised sports racing cars, many drivers were going about things in a much more professional manner, at least by the standards of the day.

Cooper Climax T39

The 'Bobtail' was the first rear-engined Cooper sports car and the progenitor of the championship-winning Cooper F1 cars. Though seen with Connaught and Bristol engines, it was the Coventry Climax unit which in both 1100cc and 1500cc form brought success to the T39. Designed by Owen Maddock, there was a resemblance to the streamlined 500cc record-breaking Cooper of earlier years. Indeed, John Cooper had used that car to test out the feasibility of the proposed new design. Cooper followed Kieft in putting the driver at the centre of the car with a tiny passenger seat to the side to meet the regulations. The engine also sat on the centre line of the car and the whole was clad in a smooth body, notable for its abrupt ending. Maddox had read the theories of a German professor who proposed that if you cut off the rear of an aerofoil and caused the air to flow correctly, it would behave as if the missing section was still there, giving the benefit of the full aerofoil effect without carrying the length and weight. The Kamm-tail has often been seen since. The car was an immediate success and led the small sports racing car revolution until first Colin Chapman's Lotus Eleven and then Eric Broadley's Lola Mk 1 came along. In the meantime Cooper had turned the Bobtail into a single-seater which would beat the world in 1959–60.

Keith Greene sets up his Cooper Climax T39 for Woodcote Corner, 22 April 1957.

Frank Nichols in the prototype Elva leads one of the most successful specials, the RWG of Roy Watling Greenwood, driven here by Mark Lund. *(26/3/55)*

From RAF Halton comes the commanding officer G. Carill-Worsley in the Halton Buckler. A Tojeiro is later added to the stable. *(26/3/55)*

Powering out of the chicane, Archie Scott Brown in Lister Bristol BHL2 is winner of the 2000cc sports car race. *(11/4/55)*

Fastest in practice and first on the road, Mike Sparken's Ferrari 750 Monza was relegated to second through a penalty for a jumped start. *(11/4/55)*

The Ferrari 750 Monza
of Luigi Piotti, slower
than expected, could
only manage 13th on
the grid and retired
from the race.
(11/4/55)

Paul Emery drives his
own Emeryson. The
car was elegant and
well finished but never
a challenger for top F1
honours. (11/4/55
Author's collection)

Cyril Wick in the original Cooper Jaguar T33, not the most attractive of the Cooper firm's products. *(11/4/55)*

Allan Moore driving Ormsby Issard-Davies's customer model Lister Bristol BHL3. *(30/5/55)*

A Le Mans start for the Johnson's Challenge Trophy race. Nearest the camera is Thomas's Jaguar XK120. *(30/5/55)*

The over 2000cc sports car race and John Heath's HWM Jaguar leads Peter Blond's Jaguar C-type 052 and Cyril Wick's Cooper Jaguar T33. *(30/5/55)*

The start of the Chichester Cup FL race. Peter Collins has the BRM on pole with Stirling Moss (Maserati 250F), Roy Salvadori (Maserati 250F) and Don Beauman (Connaught A) to his left. This picture rewards study of the crowd, officials, buildings and background. *(11/4/55 Author's collection)*

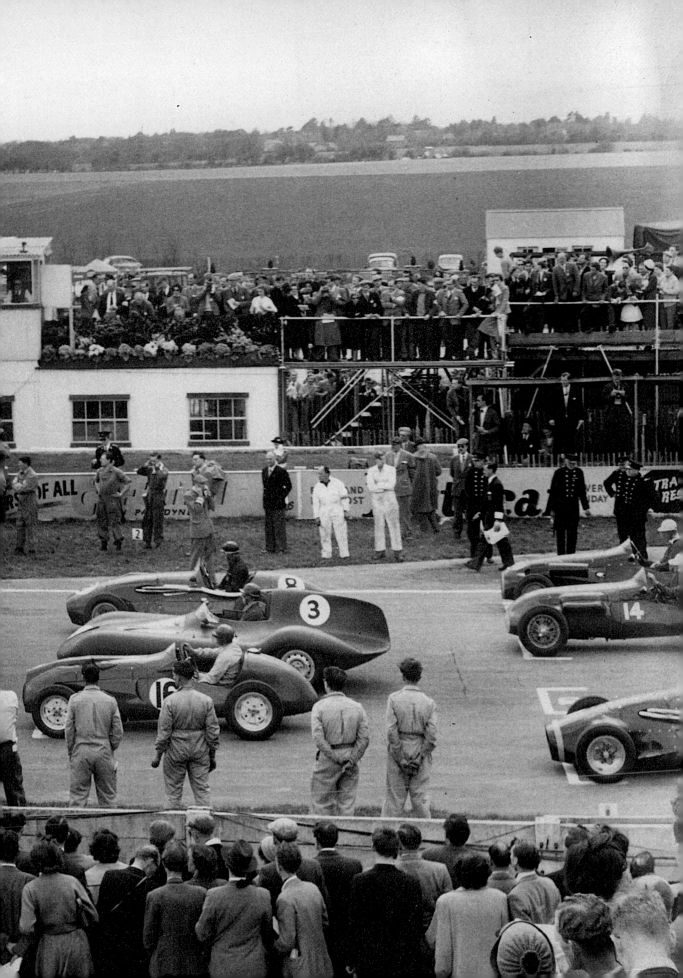

Start of the 1250cc
sports car race with
Tommy Sopwith
(Cooper Climax T39)
on pole position,
Adrian Liddell's
Buckler and Tom
Barnard's Lotus VI
alongside. *(18/6/55)*

Winner of the
1500–3500cc sports
car race, George
Abecassis drives the
latest version of the
Jaguar-engined
sports HWM.
(18/6/55)

Jeff Sparrowe's MG
Special at St Mary's
before retiring from
the handicap race for
closed cars. *(18/6/55)*

Michael MacDowel in
his Ford-powered
Lotus IX/85, fourth in
the 1250cc scratch race
and fifth in his
handicap race.
(18/6/55)

There were at least two Lester Coupés built. Compare Mike Llewellyn's No.33 (*below*) with that of Edgar Poole (*above*) and note headlights and rear windows, doors and wheel arches. (*18/6/55*)

The works supported Ferrari
750 Monzas in the Nine Hours
Race: Hawthorn/de Portago
0498M (6), Wharton/Jonneret
0514M (7), Schell/Lucas 0440M
(8). *(20/8/55)*

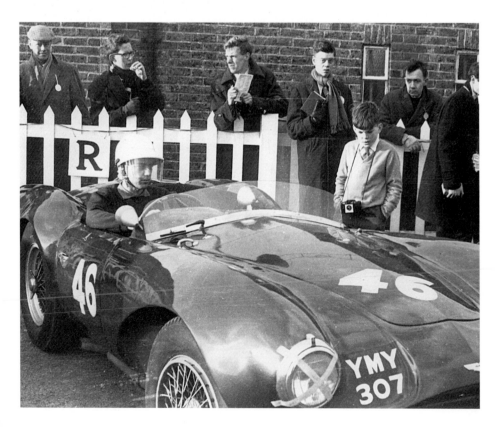

Dennis Barthel in the
original Aston Martin
DB3S/1, fifth in the
1500–3500cc sports car
race. *(24/9/55)*

Peter Collins
(1931–1958)

Graduating from 500cc F3, Peter Collins became Stirling Moss's team mate with HWM for 1952–53, racing all over the continent with the adventurous British F2 stable. In the same period he was a member of the Aston Martin sports car team, winning the 1952 Goodwood Nine Hours and the 1953 Tourist Trophy, both with Pat Griffith. Tony Vandervell put him behind the wheel of his Ferrari Thin Wall Special in 1954, and also gave him the original Vanwall to drive in its early races. BRM snapped him up for 1955 but their P25 did not arrive until the season's end. He did have the chance to exercise the V16 T15 in its final races and also to use their interim Maserati 250F. He also shared the winning Mercedes-Benz 300SLR with Stirling Moss in the Targa Florio. BRM could offer nothing to keep him from a Ferrari drive in 1956. In a team led by Fangio, Collins managed to win Grands Prix in Belgium and France. In the days when drivers could share a car, Collins handed his over to Fangio at both Monaco and Monza. The latter particularly endeared him to Enzo Ferrari since Collins was giving up his own outside chance of winning the championship. 1957 saw him joined in the Ferrari team by his great friend Mike Hawthorn, but they could do nothing to prevent Fangio, now at Maserati, from taking his fifth and final world title. The following year saw him winning the British Grand Prix at Silverstone in the new Ferrari Dino 246 as he and Hawthorn romped through the season, locked in conflict with the Vanwalls. Tragedy struck at the Nurburgring, where Collins crashed while chasing Tony Brooks in the Vanwall. He failed to recover from serious head injuries. It is said that Enzo Ferrari always held dear the memory of the handsome, charming Peter Collins.

Peter Collins in his early days, well turned out as driver of F3 Cooper.

1956

AFTER THE tragic accident in the Nine Hours Race, it was particularly cruel that on the first lap of the first race at the Easter meeting yet another driver should lose his life. Bert Rogers had rolled a Tojeiro at Lavant Corner in the Nine Hours and did the same thing again, without the previous occasion's lucky escape. The race mixed single-seaters of the old F2 with more modern sports racers, including Roy Salvadori's works Cooper T39 'Bobtail', powered by the new Coventry Climax 1470cc engine, which won from Bob Gerard's Cooper Bristol T23.

Stirling Moss had an outing in the Gilby Engineering Aston Martin DB3S and beat George Abecassis in the HWM by 23 seconds over 15 laps, despite giving away half a litre to the Jaguar-engined car. Tragedy struck yet again when Duncan Hamilton's second D-type Jaguar crashed at the end of the straight, the driver Anthony Dennis losing his life in the ensuing fire. Roy Salvadori won his second event of the day in the 1500cc sports car race. Making its debut was Colin Chapman's latest creation, the Lotus Eleven (no more model designation by Roman numerals). Reg Bicknell managed to come home fourth against the larger-engined opposition. The Eleven would confirm Chapman's position as the leading manufacturer of production sports racing cars.

The Richmond Trophy F1 race was extended to 32 laps or 77 miles. Stirling Moss brought a works Maserati 250F, the car in which he would later win the Monaco Grand Prix. Gordini was tempted across from France with one of his traditional slipper-bodied T16s for Elie Bayol and a new 8-cylinder T32 for Robert Manzon. Sir Alfred Owen had managed to attract the dream team of Mike Hawthorn and Tony Brooks, though both would become disillusioned with the new T25 2½-litre F1 car. The new Vanwalls were not ready but Connaught, boosted by Brooks's win in the Syracuse Grand Prix, brought three cars for Archie Scott Brown, Les Leston and Bob Gerard. Rob Walker's Connaught was driven by Reg Parnell, while Roy Salvadori was back with the Gilby Maserati 250F. Another French visitor, Louis Rosier, brought his own Maserati 250F and Ferrari 500/625 for Ken Wharton to drive.

Twelve F1 cars hardly constituted a large field but it produced a good race. Hawthorn took off like a rocket with Scott Brown and Moss on his tail. Both passed the BRM and all three circulated in close company and at high speed until Scott Brown slowed on lap 16 and retired on the following tour. He had succeeded in holding Moss at bay and his retirement was a great disappointment. The crowd was horrified to see an ambulance on the track yet again, but thankfully Mike Hawthorn suffered only minor hurt when the BRM somersaulted off the road at Fordwater. Brooks had been charging through the field in the second BRM but his race ended with no oil pressure.

Salvadori inherited second place behind the Moss Maserati and was followed home by the three Connaughts of Leston, Gerard and Parnell. Manzon was best of the Continentals in sixth place. Both Connaught and BRM had been able to race Moss and Maserati on equal terms but not to last the distance.

On Whit Monday, the sun shone brightly upon a duel that passed into mythology. Ivor Bueb had bought both a Cooper Climax T39 and a Lotus Climax 11 for his team, Ecurie Demi Litre. Bueb was the winner of the fateful 1955 Le Mans race, co-driving with Mike Hawthorn, and he was pleased to enter the Lotus for Hawthorn to drive when his international commitments allowed. Lotus creator Colin Chapman was a driver of considerable ability and still found time to exercise that skill on the circuits. They found themselves opposed in the opening 1500cc race, mixing it with Jack Brabham, Michael MacDowel, Cliff Allison, Reg Bicknell, Alan Stacey and a dozen others. Last on the grid was Air Commodore Donald 'Pathfinder' Bennett in his own creation, the Fairthorpe Electron.

Though Bicknell led at the start, Hawthorn was in front by the start of lap two and Chapman relieved him of that lead on lap three. Hawthorn tried every trick in his considerable repertoire to get past Chapman. First on one side and then the other, his car would nose alongside and then be forced to drop back. Then he darted up the inside at Woodcote on lap four. Coming through Fordwater, the two protagonists started to catch the backmarkers and passed a startled Bennett, one on each side. Chapman repeated Hawthorn's own trick by darting up the inside at Woodcote, Hawthorn re-took him and was then himself passed once again. Just for a change Hawthorn then accelerated up the outside of Chapman at Woodcote to lead on lap eight, only to be re-passed on lap nine. Hawthorn was back in front on lap 11 and it was Chapman's turn to lead on lap 12. They were circulating in such close company that it was inevitable that the pair would touch. It happened at Madgwick and sent both cars into a spin. Hawthorn decided that discretion was called for and visited the pits to check for damage. Though he rejoined still in second place, Chapman was not to be caught and ran out the winner of a memorable contest.

The over-1500cc race was something of an anticlimax as Bob Berry won easily in Broadhead's D-type Jaguar from the three Ecurie Ecosse cars. It was a sign of the times that the Formule Libre race attracted only four F2 cars to mix with the fastest of the sports cars. Berry set off in the lead followed by Chapman, promising yet another exciting contest until the Lotus lost second gear before Madgwick. Then, on lap three, the Jaguar got away from Berry at Fordwater. The car ploughed through two fences and then somersaulted into a field, throwing out the driver, who broke his ankle. Ron Flockhart's Ecosse D-type Jaguar took on the lead and held it until throwing a tyre tread on the very last lap, letting through Desmond Titterington's similar car to win and Hawthorn into second place.

The Members' Meetings were beset by authority when it was ordered that any car leaving the track with all four wheels or spinning so that the rear wheels overtook the front (except when avoiding an accident) would be excluded. This rule resulted in many disqualifications and not a few disgruntled drivers.

With no Nine Hours Race, the season wound up with another sports car/Formula 3 meeting along the lines of the Whitsun event. Among the 1500cc sports cars appeared Roy Salvadori in the prototype works Cooper Climax T41, built for the new Formula 2 which was due to start in 1957. This car sired the series of F1 and F2 Coopers which would reach the greatest heights over the next four years. It also won the Woodcote Cup and Sussex Trophy races on this pleasant September afternoon and it seemed that Roy Salvadori would complete his hat-trick with victory in the Goodwood Trophy for sports cars over 1500cc. He was driving the latest works Aston Martin DB3S, but found himself beaten by Tony Brooks in an older DB3S (the car that had won the 1955 Nine Hours) who recorded his first win for Aston Martin.

The final meeting saw the *Motor Sport* Brooklands trophy awarded to Peter Lumsden (Lotus Climax Mk IX). The new Lotus Eleven was appearing in large numbers by the season's end, driven by such men as Bill Frost, Alan Stacey, Keith Hall, Cliff Allison and Innes Ireland.

John Ogier's Jaguar XK120 is the worse for wear. *(17/3/56)*

Start of the opening race for racing and sports cars under 2000cc. Salvadori's 1470cc Cooper Climax T39 faces the starter with Bob Gerard (Cooper Bristol T23), Cliff Davis (Lotus Bristol Mk X) and John Young (Connaught A-type). *(2/4/56)*

Louis Cornet's new Maserati 150S, which lost its showroom-fresh appearance when it assaulted the chicane. *(2/4/56)*

Works Connaughts for (*front*) Les Leston chassis B1 (7) and (*back*) Archie Scott Brown chassis B2 (6). *(2/4/56)*

A victorious Stirling
Moss converts Maserati
250F 2522 into a two-
seater to transport
Archie Scott Brown to
the paddock after the
Glover Trophy Race.
(2/4/56)

The eight-cylinder Gordini
T32 0041 driven to sixth in
the Glover Trophy race by
Robert Manzon. *(2/4/56)*

King Hussein of Jordan
tries a Cooper Climax
T39, possibly at one of
the BARC general
practice days.

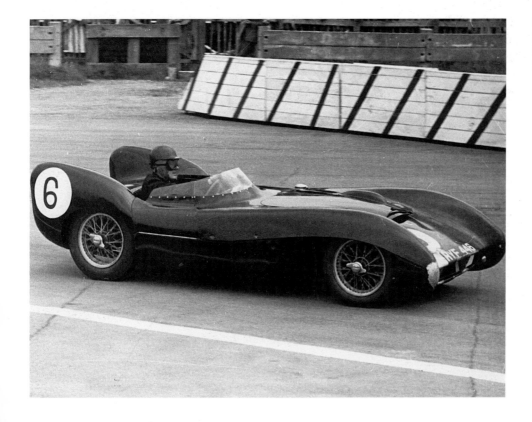

Lotus Mk IX (130) of
Peter Lumsden, fourth
in the 1250cc scratch
race. *(7/7/56)*

George Livanos
finished fifth in the
1500–3500cc scratch
race in the left-hand
drive Aston Martin
DB2/4. *(7/7/56)*

The check shirt helps
to identify Cliff Davis,
second in the
1500–3500cc race in
his Lotus Bristol Mk
IX/90. *(7/7/56)*

Dick Prior's Lotus VI
finds Ken MacKenzies'
Elva Climax Mk 1
spinning in its path.
(7/7/56)

The start of the
Goodwood Trophy
race with Noel
Cunningham Reid's
HWM Jaguar on pole.
Next to him is Tony
Brooks' Aston Martin
DB3S about to record
his first win for the
marque. Alongside are
Roy Salvadori
(DB3S/9) and Ron
Flockhart in Ecurie
Ecosse D-type Jaguar
XKD501. *(8/9/56)*

The prototype Formula 2 Cooper Climax T41 driven by Roy Salvadori to two wins. This car led directly to Cooper's world championship-winning cars. *(8/9/56)*

The Woodcote Cup race with winner Roy Salvadori on pole. Reg Bicknell's Lotus 11 has the Coopers of Les Leston and Michael MacDowel beside him. *(8/9/56)*

Lotus Climax Eleven

With 10 projects behind him, Colin Chapman's eleventh creation was to be his most successful both in race results and the order book. The Coventry Climax engine was in good supply in 1100cc form and becoming more freely available as a 1½-litre unit. The chassis followed the form of its predecessor, the Mk IX, but was more compact and refined. Originally available as 'Le Mans', 'Club' and 'Sports' to different specifications, the most popular was the Le Mans built to full race trim. Most private owners opted for the Climax FWA 1098cc engine as the 1460cc FWB added over £200 to the price. The Eleven's introduction coincided with Cooper's entry into F2 and though honours were shared with the Cooper T39 in 1956, the Eleven took over the prime position in its class until the arrival of the Lola Mk 1 in 1959. With the decline of 500cc F3, the smaller engined sports cars became the 'entry level' class and there were plenty of races at all ability levels on circuits all over Europe. The works 1100cc car of Reg Bicknell and Peter Jopp won their class at the 1956 Le Mans. In 1957 Lotus introduced the 'Mark 2' with suspension borrowed from the new F2 Twelve and an option for the new Climax FPF twin-cam engine. At Le Mans, Lotus Elevens finished first, second and fourth in the 1100cc class and won the 750cc class and with it the Index of Performance prize. The French had always collared this with their small-engined devices and were none too pleased. 1958 saw Chapman occupied with the Fifteen (an Eleven on steroids) but, in private hands, the Eleven remained the backbone of club racing.

Bill Frost in one of the earliest Lotus Elevens (154), second in the 1250cc scratch race on 7 July 1956.

Louis Rosier (1905–1956)

From the French Auvergne, Louis Rosier raced motorcycles and cars before the war but made his name in post-war events. From his garage business in Clermont-Ferrand he won the 1947 Albi GP in his Talbot. This was followed by a succession of high place finishes and the purchase for 1948 of a new 4½-litre Lago Talbot. With this slow but reliable car he finished in the first four in five major races and won the Salon GP. 1949 saw him win the Belgian GP at Spa which, together with another series of high placings, made him champion of France for the first of four consecutive years. Never the quickest he was nonetheless consistent, adding the Dutch and Albi GPs over the next three years. In 1950 he took a re-bodied Talbot to victory at Le Mans, driving for 20 of the 24 hours, sharing with his son Jean-Claude. Switching to Ferrari in 1952, he won at Albi and Cadours. With Talbot he finished fifth in the 1953 Carrera Panamericana. With Maserati 250F and Ferrari 500 he raced on under the new F1 but with less success. He lost his life aged 50 in the 1956 Montlhéry Coupe du Salon when his sports Ferrari overturned, a cruel end for a driver who had achieved so much through guile and consistency rather than driving on the ragged edge.

Louis Rosier, French veteran and Ferrari driver.

1957

'At the start I managed to stall it on the grid right there in front of 55,000 people'
Graham Hill

THERE WAS doubt as to whether there would be any racing in 1957. The Suez Crisis threatened oil supplies and the Goodwood season did not start until the Easter meeting on 22 April. For the first time there was no handicap race in the programme.

Cooper was not only ready for the new Formula 2, but had also developed the prototype T41 into the improved T43 production car. Works drivers Roy Salvadori and Jack Brabham were seen off by Tony Brooks in Rob Walker's T41. Lotus only managed to get one type 12 to the line for Cliff Allison. This was the first single-seater racing Lotus, but it retired after only four laps. Another debutant was Graham Hill, in his first drive in a large single-seater, behind the wheel of Tommy Atkins's A-type Connaught with its 2-litre engine reduced to 1500cc.

The Vanwall had caused a sensation with Stirling Moss's win in the 1956 Silverstone International Trophy and a series of fruitless but encouraging drives throughout the season by Harry Schell. Tony Vandervell employed Colin Chapman to sort out the original chassis and he in turn had brought in aerodynamicist Frank Costin, who developed the distinctive teardrop bodywork which would become so familiar. That Mr Vandervell really meant business became clear when he engaged Stirling Moss and Tony Brooks as his drivers for 1957, a pairing which must be one of the motor-racing dream teams of all time.

BRM was still struggling with the T25 first raced in 1955, Roy Salvadori and Ron Flockhart not having the most enjoyable time with the cars. Also struggling, but through lack of finance, was Connaught. Archie Scott Brown remained faithful and they had recruited young Stuart Lewis-Evans to bolster the team. The Vanwalls were plainly the quickest with Moss and Brooks taking the first two positions on the grid. Carrying his favourite race number '7', Moss created an unassailable lead from which he was forced to retire on lap 13 when his throttle linkage broke. This problem had occurred before. Indeed Brooks had been forced to pit with the same malaise, but the mechanics had effected a repair and sent him back out to record a few more racing miles and have a crack at the lap record.

He obliged with 96.43mph. Scott Brown had also retired and Lewis-Evans was left to drive a cool-headed race to victory over Jack Fairman in Rob Walker's Connaught. Third came Ron Flockhart in the evil-handling BRM (which was also later to benefit from Colin Chapman's advice). In fourth place came Jack Brabham in the F2 Cooper and fifth the old faithful (though re-chassised and re-bodied) Maserati 250F of Gilby Engineering, driven by Jim Russell.

Salvadori and Brooks were back with works Aston Martins, Brooks in a DB3S but Salvadori in the DBR1 as first produced with a 2½-litre engine. Way down the grid was Archie Scott Brown in Brian Lister's latest creation, a reconstruction of his original MG-engined car to house a 3.4 Jaguar unit. Sixth soon after the start, Archie led by the end of the first lap and won the race by over 21 seconds from Salvadori and Brooks. Fourth was Duncan Hamilton in his newly acquired long-nosed D-type Jaguar.

The new 1½-litre Coventry Climax engine was finding its way into sports cars and Colin Chapman used one in his Lotus Eleven to win the 1500cc race. Stuart Lewis-Evans completed a good day by winning the 500cc F3 race.

Innes Ireland was starring in the Members' Meetings with opposition from Chris Bristow and Keith Greene, son of Sid Greene of Gilby Engineering.

Michael Head won the feature race at the Whitsun meeting in his Cooper Jaguar from Peter Blond in Tommy Atkins's Aston Martin DB3S. Alan Stacey beat a field including eight other Lotus Elevens in the 1100cc race. A handicap for Bentley cars saw an impressive drive from George Burton, who got up to fourth place from a scratch start. Bob Bradley was also pressing really hard even after collecting a large section of chicane fencing in his front suspension. He finished the race in fifth place but had the bad luck to turn the Bentley over at Woodcote on the slowing down lap. However, he did have the good luck to be able to walk away once it had been lifted off him. Donald Day won the race in his 1925 3-litre.

Stuart Lewis-Evans started the September meeting where he left off at Easter – by winning the 500cc F3 race. Connaught had been defeated by their financial troubles, the works cars sold and their drivers dispersed. Lewis-Evans had been snapped up by Tony Vandervell to join Moss and Brooks in the Vanwall team.

If the small sports car races were full of Lotus Elevens, the F2 grids were overflowing with Coopers. Roy Salvadori and Jack Brabham were the works drivers, while Rob Walker's two cars were driven on this occasion by Tony Brooks and Jack Fairman. Speedway star Ronnie Moore came over from New Zealand with Ray Thackwell, racing Cooper T43s as Kiwi Equipe. Works Lotus 12s for Graham Hill, Cliff Allison and Keith Hall joined Archie Scott Brown in the second of only three single-seater Listers ever built, none of which found any success. Salvadori and Brabham fought a race-long duel and, although the Australian came off worse, he set a new class record at 96.00mph, which was only 0.4 seconds over Brooks's outright circuit record.

After his disappointment with the F2 car, Scott Brown made amends with victory in the large sports car race. Indeed, he was beaten only once during the 1957 season. Duncan Hamilton was a little too enthusiastic at the Le Mans start and spun through 180 degrees, causing alarm among those around him.

It was unimaginable only a few years earlier, but Stirling Moss in the Vanwall won the Italian Grand Prix at Monza. What is more, the Italians had put on a second Grand Prix that year, at Pescara, and Moss had won that too. Tony Vandervell had seen his dream come true. Not only had he beaten 'those bloody red cars' but he'd done it on their own home ground – twice in a month. Add to this the emotional victory in the British Grand Prix at Aintree and it is easy to see why the British enthusiast was eager to applaud Moss as he demonstrated the Monza-winning car in a 10-lap attempt at the Goodwood lap record. The car was war-weary and broke a valve on the fifth lap, but it did equal the lap record on lap four.

Herbert McKay Fraser in the works Series 2 Lotus 11 with 1475cc Climax engine. *(22/4/57)*

The Connaught B3 was variously known as Moby Dick and the Toothpaste Tube. Winner of the Glover Trophy, it was driven by Stuart Lewis-Evans. *(22/4/57)*

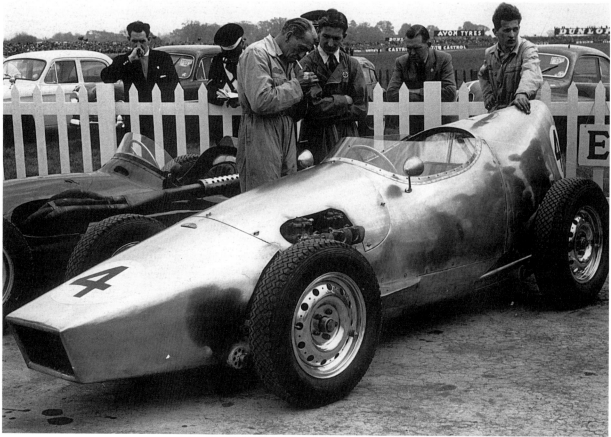

Archie Scott Brown did drive sports cars other than Listers on occasion. Here he wheels the works Elva Climax Mk 2 through the chicane. *(22/4/57)*

Start of the Glover Trophy race with Moss, Brooks, Scott Brown and Flockhart on the front row. Next comes Salvadori in the new high-cockpit BRM, Fairman in Rob Walker's Connaught, now with Syracuse bodywork, the Emeryson and Brabham's F2 Cooper. The only foreign car, Jim Russell's Gilby Maserati, has been left behind. *(22/4/57)*

The Gilby Engineering Maserati 250F driven by Jim Russell is nearing the end of its F1 career. *(22/4/57)*

Ron Flockhart managed to bring the ill-handling BRM home in third place. *(22/4/57)*

Graham Hill had driven a 500cc car before but this was his first race in a grown-up single-seater. The Connaught A3 had its engine reduced to 1500cc for the new F2. *(22/4/57)*

Christian Goethal's Porsche at cross purpose in Woodcote Corner. Note the the roof behind him did not always carry Shell advertising. *(22/4/57)*

Colin Chapman driving Lotus Eleven 308 with a borrowed nose following Mac Fraser's earlier argument with the chicane. Following is Ron Flockhart in John Coombs's Lotus Eleven. *(22/4/57)*

Innes Ireland, winner of the 1500cc Sports Car Race, tours in on his lap of honour. *(31/8/57)*

Alan Stacey leads Innes
Ireland and Keith
Greene. Peter
Ashdown, Robbie
Mackenzie-Low and
Jack Westcott follow
on. *(28/9/57)*

Fred Marriott's Lotus
VI/41, Climax-engined
and working hard.
(28/9/57)

Archie Scott Brown's works Lister Climax was the firm's second attempt at an F2 car. It was not a success and was not seen again after Archie's untimely death. *(28/9/57)*

This F2 Cooper Climax T43 was entered by Alan Brown for Jim Russell. *(28/9/57)*

Vanwall

Disenchantment with the BRM effort led Tony Vandervell to throw the resources of his V.P. Ltd into producing his own car. After five years racing modified Ferraris as 'Thinwall Specials' (named after the thin wall bearings that his firm produced), the first Vanwall appeared in 1954. Modified for 1955 but completely rebuilt for 1956 with redesign directed by Colin Chapman and Frank Costin, the cars finally came into their own in 1957, winning GPs at Aintree, Monza and Pescara. In 1958 they swept the board, winning six out of nine GPs and taking the inaugural Constructors' Championship. Stirling Moss missed the world championship by a single point. The strain had taken its toll on Vandervell's health and he was advised to retire his team. He raced a single car occasionally over the next three years, including the rear-engined VW14, but the full racing team was never reconstituted. On his death in 1967 V.P. Ltd was taken over by GKN, who kept the Thinwall, the rear-engined car and two Vanwalls. The whole collection was sold to Tom Wheatcroft at Donington Park in 1968. He has retained VW9 and reconstructed the unraced streamlined VW6. He also retained the Thinwall and rear-engined car. VW10 was sold, as was the rebuilt amalgamation of VW5/VW11. The cars appear regularly at historic events, reminders of the most important team in Britain's march to the front of GP racing.

Tony Brooks tells Tony Vandervell just how the Vanwall is behaving while John Bolster awaits his turn to ask a few questions.

Archie Scott Brown (1927–1958)

Archie was born with a malformed right hand and short, distorted legs. Not deterred by these handicaps, he started racing an MG TD. Among his opponents was Brian Lister, owner of a fearsome JAP-engined Tojeiro. Realising Archie's talent, Lister asked him to drive the car and the resulting successes encouraged the development of the first MG-engined Lister. This was followed by Bristol, Maserati and Jaguar-engined cars, all of which saw victory with Archie behind the wheel. Initially he was refused race entries but there were many voices raised in support and, once he was able to demonstrate his skill, there was no restriction to his racing, at least within the UK. He drove for Elva in 1956 and in the same year drove for the works Connaught F1 team. It was the Jaguar-engined Lister that brought his greatest successes. He won on just about every British circuit, defeating everyone who was anyone. Bested by Masten Gregory in the Ecurie Ecosse Lister Jaguar at Silverstone, he was dicing with the same driver and car at Spa when he went off the wet road and died in the ensuing fire. His death was a great shock to British enthusiasts and Brian Lister continued with his team only reluctantly. Physical handicap and supreme car control rarely go together but Archie Scott Brown was an exceptional man.

Archie Scott Brown in the B-type Connaught.

1958

THE CIRCUIT was not quiet through the winter. A vehicle subway near the pits was to take traffic beneath the circuit and into the paddock, where new roofed stalls were built. There was a new tunnel beneath the Lavant Straight to take pedestrians to new enclosures on the infield where there were also two new grass landing strips for light aircraft.

It had been six years since Mike Hawthorn burst onto the international motor racing scene with his spectacular wins at the 1952 Easter Goodwood. The following year as a works Ferrari driver he won his first Grand Prix. Flirtations with BRM and Vanwall proved fruitless and he repeatedly gravitated back to the Italian team. For 1958 Ferrari produced the Dino 246 and entered one for Hawthorn to drive in the Glover Trophy. BRM had employed Jean Behra and Harry Schell to drive the much-improved T25s.

Vanwall were absent. Both Tony Vandervell and BARC general secretary John Morgan were strong characters. Vandervell was not over-fond of Goodwood as a circuit and the negotiations for his cars to appear always led to lively correspondence and telephone conversations, during which there were free and frank exchanges of views. However, it was more likely the protracted task of converting the Vanwalls to the newly mandatory pump fuel that kept them away rather than a wrangle over cash. This may have been just as well since Vandervell might have been looking for the £1,000 per car which it was rumoured that Ferrari would be paid.

With no Vanwall available Stirling Moss was free to drive Rob Walker's Cooper Climax. This combination had just set the Grand Prix world on its ear by winning the Argentine Grand Prix against the full might of the Italian teams. The Climax engine had been stretched to 1960cc for the Walker and works cars of Roy Salvadori and Jack Brabham, although there were not enough to go round and the third car of Ian Burgess had the 1490cc F2 unit.

Both Connaught and Maserati were no longer entering F1 as works cars.

The Connaughts had been sold at auction, two going to Mr Bernard Ecclestone, who employed Archie Scott Brown and his friend Stuart Lewis-Evans as drivers. Racing motorcyclist Keith Campbell had an ex-works Maserati 250F and Bruce Halford had the Prince Bira car which had actually swapped chassis with the Owen (BRM) 250F.

For the first time the F1 race was over 42 laps, more than 100 miles. As the flag fell, the Moss Cooper stalled and Behra's BRM led away from Brabham's Cooper and Hawthorn's Ferrari. Moss finally got away to such good effect that he was eighth at the end of the first lap. Hawthorn was up to second when Behra approached the chicane on lap five, only to find his brakes inoperative. Having already turned to the right he was heading straight for the spectators on the inside of the circuit. Bravely he heaved the car to the left and demolished both chicane wall and BRM. The crowd was amazed to see him hauled from the wreck without serious hurt. Raymond Mays reported: 'Now I had to take another ride in the ambulance to Chichester hospital, to take Jean for examination. Last time it had been to accompany Mike Hawthorn.'

Moss passed Brabham for second place on the tenth lap and set off after Hawthorn, hounding him until the Climax engine gave out on lap 22. During their dice they had each broken the lap record and left it to their joint credit at 97.30mph. Brabham came home second with Salvadori's Cooper third and Cliff Allison's works Lotus 12 fourth. But, of course, these Cooper and Lotus devices were not really F1 cars. Moss's Argentine victory was marvellous, yes, but something of a fluke. The pundits started to revise their opinions when Trintignant took the Monaco Grand Prix in Rob Walker's Cooper and 1959 would complete the revolution.

It was hoped that Ferrari would bring a Testa Rossa for the sports car race. They did rather better and produced a brand new 2-litre Dino sports model for Peter Collins to drive. Equipe Nationale Belge turned up with two of the exciting pontoon-fendered 3-litre Testa Rossas for Willy Mairesse and Lucien Bianchi. Colin Chapman produced a new chassis, the Lotus 15, to make use of the larger Climax engine. Graham Hill put the first example on fourth spot for the Le Mans start in the face of many larger cars including Lister Jaguars for Archie Scott Brown, Peter Whitehead and Bruce Halford. Fastest in practice was Stirling Moss with the works Aston Martin 3.8-litre DBR2 and he was soon to wrest the lead from Scott Brown. Archie fought back gamely despite giving away half a litre. The cushion which supported his back had slipped onto the seat at the Le Mans start and he was having some trouble controlling the car when the steering broke on lap 10. Moss was then untroubled by Collins, whose 2-litre car was some way behind.

Coopers dominated the F2 race, at least in numbers. Brabham's works car won but the Lotus 12s of Graham Hill and Cliff Allison were second and third.

In fact Hill had led for some distance until Brabham went round the outside at Woodcote and somehow emerged in front.

Stuart Lewis-Evans had won the F3 race yet again with a young Trevor Taylor in second place. Motor racing in the fifties was a cruel sport. Stuart Lewis-Evans, Archie Scott Brown, Peter Whitehead and Peter Collins would not survive the 1958 season.

Goodwood is always remembered as bathed in sunshine. As many of its meetings took place on Bank Holidays, which are traditionally wet, memory is probably selective. Whit Monday, 26 May 1958, was certainly wet though the afternoon brightened somewhat. What were known as series production cars were given their own race series by *Autosport* magazine, providing exercise for AC Bristols, Triumph TR2s and TR3s, Morgans, Austin Healeys and Frazer Nash. Ted Whiteaway in one of Ken Rudd's ACs won the opening race and this was followed by a gaggle of ERAs in the Historic Racing Car event. Bill Moss won in R5B. The main race went to Graham Whitehead's customer model Lister Jaguar.

Saloon car racing was becoming popular and the Jaguar 3.4 was the car to beat with the Austin A35 cleaning up in the smaller class. The Jaguars succeeded again with Duncan Hamilton first in John Coombs's car and Tommy Sopwith and Sir Gawaine Baillie second and third in the Equipe Endeavour cars. John Sprinzel's Speedwell A35 won the 1000cc class. Perhaps more surprising was the Hillman Minx, winner of the 1500cc class with Barney Everley behind the wheel.

Michael Taylor and Keith Greene had fought a season-long battle in their Lotus Elevens. Competition for the Brooklands Trophy extended to the final meeting of the season and Taylor took the championship in the last race.

The RAC had invited the BARC to revive the Tourist Trophy race, not run since 1955 when fatal accidents had marred the Dundrod event. Doubtless remembering their experiences with the Nine Hours Race, they agreed to a four-hour event which would count for half points in the World Manufacturers' Championship series. Though Ferrari and Equipe Nationale Belge entered cars, they all failed to appear, leaving only the two works Porsches to justify the 'international' tag, drawn by the prospect of beating Aston Martin to second place in the championship which Ferrari had already won.

Aston Martin had a proud record to defend as winners of all three Nine Hours Races. They had all three Vanwall drivers, Stirling Moss sharing with Tony Brooks and Stuart Lewis-Evans with American Carroll Shelby. The third car was shared by the Cooper drivers Roy Salvadori and Jack Brabham. Brian Lister was deeply shocked by the death of Archie Scott Brown at Spa earlier in the year. With a heavy heart he decided to continue with the team and entered two cars for Bruce Halford/Ivor Bueb and New Zealander Ross Jensen with John Bekaert. Ecurie Ecosse entered just one D-type Jaguar for Innes Ireland/Masten Gregory.

The 2-litre entry was headed by the works Porsches, an RSK for Jean Behra and Edgar Barth and an older RS for Karel de Beaufort and Bino Heins (yes, really). They were opposed by three Lotus 15s, a Lotus 11, the Le Mans AC Bristol and Dick Jacobs's MG A Twin Cam.

The 1100cc class was crowded with Lotus Elevens but there were also three Elvas and the prototype Lola Mk 1, driven by its designer Eric Broadley and Peter Gammon. The Lola was particularly impressive though lost a lot of time with a puncture and no spare wheels.

A fine day in early autumn brought out a good crowd. Aston Martin filled the first three places at the Le Mans start followed by the Bueb/Halford Lister Jaguar and the Graham Hill/Cliff Allison Lotus Climax 15. As was usual, Moss was first out of the starting blocks with Shelby and Salvadori close on his heels. On the tenth lap Salvadori slid wide at Madgwick and pushed Edward Greenall's Lotus 15 off course. Shelby avoided the mêlée but Bueb left the road in the Lister and bent his steering. Salvadori called at the pits for a check over and then hurried through the pack to retake third place.

After the driver changes, the Aston Martin team continued on its impressive way in the order Brooks, Lewis-Evans and Brabham, and the order remained the same when the number one drivers retook control. They were followed by the Behra/Barth Porsche but there was nothing that the German team could do to prevent Aston Martin taking the first three places and thereby securing joint second position with Porsche in the Manufacturers' Championship.

The season closed with the 32nd Members' Meeting which, unusually, included a 500cc F3 won by Tommy Bridger, a fine driver who on this day beat a field including Don Parker and Trevor Taylor.

Australian motorcycle
racer Keith Campbell
in his ex-works
Maserati 250F 2526.
(7/4/58)

A rare sighting of an
Aston Martin DB3S
Coupé. Jean Bloxam in
DB3S/120. *(26/4/58)*

From scratch to third in his five-lap handicap came Dennis Barthel in Aston Martin DB3S/5, a car previously driven by Parnell, Salvadori, Collins, Moss and Brooks. *(26/4/58)*

R.G. Brain in his Ford-engined Lotus 11 387 was no match for the Climax-engined brigade. *(26/4/58)*

Winner of the handicap race for closed cars, J. Wheeler's Austin A35 may possibly have had less tyre tread after the race than before. *(23/8/58)*

The works line-up of Aston Martins for the Tourist Trophy. Left to right: DBR1/1, DBR1/3, DBR1/2 and practice car DBR3/1 (later DBR1/4). *(13/9/58)*

The start of the TT and Stirling
Moss and Carroll Shelby are
already seated and firing up
their works Aston Martin
DBR1s, while most drivers are
still climbing aboard. *(13/9/58)*

A determined look on his face, Duncan Hamilton drives Jaguar D-type 601 to sixth in the TT. *(13/9/58)*

Compare this Ecurie Ecosse D-type Jaguar 504 (driven by Ireland and Gregory) with Hamilton's car. *(13/9/58)*

Porsche made the first Goodwood TT 'international'. Here French ace Jean Behra in the RSK he shared with Edgar Barth finishes fourth behind the Aston Martins. *(13/9/58)*

Ferrari Dino 246

Ferrari's modified Lancia D50 carried Fangio to the 1956 world championship and raced on into 1957. A new V6-engined design appeared first for F2 and then as the Dino 246 for F1 in 1958. This was to be the final front-engined Ferrari GP car, developed over the next three seasons in the face of the British rear-engined opposition. Not only was the engine at the wrong end, but Ferrari was unwilling to switch to disc brakes. The original Dino 246 was among the prettiest of all GP cars, its Scaglietti designed bodywork rivalling the Maserati 250F in its classic beauty. Mike Hawthorn's chassis '0003'

was perhaps spoilt by the old-fashioned aero screen and low-cut cockpit sides that he favoured, but that did not prevent him becoming the first British world champion in 1958. There were victories in early season races, including Goodwood, but the Grand Prix season was to be no walkover. They won at Reims and Silverstone and Hawthorn put together enough good finishes to pip Moss to the title by one point, but the season cost the lives of Luigi Musso and Peter Collins. The 1959 and 1960 developments of the car were still front runners on circuits that favoured their characteristics but they rarely beat the rear-engined brigade and Ferrari finally bowed to the inevitable and went with the flow.

Mike Hawthorn with the Ferrari Dino 246 which would carry him to the first world championship to be won by a British driver.

Mike Hawthorn
(1929–1959)

Pipe-smoking, beer-drinking, golden-haired Mike Hawthorn was the popular idea of a racing driver in the 1950s. Born in Yorkshire, the family moved to Farnham in Surrey when Mike was two. His father Leslie took over the Tourist Trophy Garage from where he tuned racing motorcycles. In 1950 the pair went racing with two Rileys and in the following year Mike won the Brooklands Memorial Trophy at Goodwood. 1952 saw his great success with the Cooper Bristol that propelled him to a works GP Ferrari seat in 1953. A good season with the Scuderia was crowned by victory over Fangio in the French GP. 1954 started badly, with burns from an accident at the Syracuse GP and controversy over his exemption from military service, and became infinitely worse when his father was killed on the journey home from the Whitsun Goodwood meeting. Vanwalls in 1955 were not the team that they would later become and Hawthorn returned to Ferrari towards the end of the season. As leader of the Jaguar sports car team he was winner of Le Mans with Ivor Bueb, but the victory was overshadowed by the accident that cost the lives of over 80 spectators. Hawthorn was widely blamed, though later exonerated. 1956 was another fruitless year, this time with BRM, but 1957 saw him back at Ferrari, this time with 'Mon Ami Mate' Peter Collins. The pair could do nothing against the great Fangio in his Maserati but 1958 was Mike's year. Despite winning only one GP, consistency brought him the world championship by a single point from his old rival Stirling Moss. The deaths of Luigi Musso, Stuart Lewis-Evans and, above all, Peter Collins convinced him to retire at the season's end, only to lose his life in a road accident a few months later.

Mike Hawthorn chats with Louise and Peter Collins and Harry Schell before his win in the Easter 1958 F1 race at the start of his last and championship-winning season.

1959

BRITAIN HAD its first world champion in Mike Hawthorn. At the end of the 1958 season he announced his retirement, only to lose his life in a road accident a few weeks later. Vanwall had won the F1 Manufacturers' Championship but the effort took its toll on Tony Vandervell's health and his doctors advised him to give up his racing team. The 1959 season would be very different. Missing would be Hawthorn, Collins, Lewis-Evans, Scott Brown, Peter Whitehead and the Vanwall team. Cooper would dominate both F1 and F2 and the Lotus Eleven would meet its match.

Eric Broadley's Lola Climax Mk 1 had impressed during the latter part of 1958. Three cars appeared in the first race at the Easter meeting, driven by Peter Ashdown, Peter Gammon and Michael Taylor. From the first three places on the grid they took the first three places in the race. Colin Chapman had understood that the Lotus Eleven was about to be eclipsed and produced the Seventeen. Two were entered and both failed to start, an inauspicious beginning for one of Chapman's least successful designs. Frank Nichols's Elva marque had now reached its fourth model, which was also capable of challenging Lotus in the 1100cc sports car class. Missing were the Coopers.

They had moved up a class with the T49 'Monaco' model which used the 2-litre Climax engine. A few even used the new 2½-litre Climax engine, which finally elevated Cooper and Lotus to proper GP status. The first of these engines appeared in the Glover Trophy F1 race powering Stirling Moss's Rob Walker Cooper T51 and the similar works cars of Jack Brabham and Masten Gregory, together with Graham Hill's Lotus 16.

Scuderia Centro Sud had filled a couple of trucks with Maseratis and trekked to Goodwood for the first time. This Italian team raced in Grands Prix throughout the 1950s and 1960s. It is tempting to call them the Minardi of their day, but the essential difference was that Centro Sud had a better chance of finishing in the money. Not only were there non-championship F1 races where the works teams may have been absent, but it was possible to improve the performance of the car through the ability of the driver. Centro Sud employed not only ambitious Italians but drivers such as Carroll Shelby, Masten Gregory and Joachim Bonnier. Gerino Gerini was entered for Goodwood but failed to appear, leaving 'Nano' da Silva Ramos to drive the Maserati 250F, which had been remodelled with a high tail somewhat reminiscent of the Vanwall. The other Centro Sud 250F was taken over by the British driver who drove just about everything during his long career, Jack Fairman. Also from Italy came another 250F for Giorgio Scarlatti.

BRM were at last succeeding with the T25 and had attracted Harry Schell and Joachim Bonnier, Schell making fastest lap in practice. Roy Salvadori was awaiting the new Aston Martin GP car. Both he and Jack Brabham had been courted by Astons, and Coopers, though anxious not to lose them, could not afford to keep both. Brabham stayed at Coopers as number one, supported by Bruce McLaren and Masten Gregory. In the meantime Salvadori drove for Tommy Atkins' High Efficiency Motors team. Knowing that the 2½-litre Coventry Climax engine would be in short supply, they used a Maserati 200S unit bored out to 2489cc.

Moss started in fifth place after practice problems but shot to second behind Schell and ahead of Brabham and Bonnier. 'The grid was drenched with rain and we scuttled off into the spray, motoring gingerly with lowered tyre pressures' Bruce McLaren said afterwards.

Ken Kavanagh spun his Maserati at the exit to the chicane, clouted the barrier and finished up at the pit road. He described the incident thus: 'On a wet track I came spinning into the pits backwards. People were injured and I decided that my car racing career was over'.

Kavanagh's 250F was one of the 1957 works lightweight cars, chassis 2527. It sat idle until 1964 when Patrick Lindsay brought it back to the UK for historic racing. Graham Hill's Lotus 16 also retired early. Moss squeezed into the lead on lap 10, Schell then being demoted to third by Brabham. And so they finished, with Moss recording fastest lap at 94.12mph.

The sports car race fell to the works Lister Jaguar, now carrying Frank Costin-designed streamlined bodywork and driven by Ivor Bueb in the lamented absence of Archie Scott Brown. Jack Brabham won the F2 Lavant Cup against the British Racing Partnership Coopers powered by Borgward engines. Jaguars swept the saloon event with another win for Ivor Bueb ahead of Roy Salvadori and Sir Gawaine Baillie, Les Leston's Riley 1.5 recording a creditable sixth ahead of the Ford Zephyrs.

Ecurie Ecosse were having to look elsewhere for their machinery, Jaguar having withdrawn from racing. They ordered cars from both Lister and Tojeiro. Ron Flockhart won the Whitsun Trophy in the Scottish team's Tojeiro

Jaguar, while Peter Blond brought their Lister Jaguar home third behind John Bekaert's similar car.

The Tourist Trophy came to Goodwood a second time on 5 September 1959. Aston Martin had won Le Mans and had the Manufacturers' Championship within their grasp. The race was to be for six hours, counting for full points and to be held on the circuit where Aston Martin had a remarkable record, having won all the long-distance sports car races held there. Both Ferrari and Porsche were in with a chance and sent full works teams, resulting in the most impressive entry for any Goodwood event thus far. In fact, the world's greatest drivers would be there.

The DBR1 Aston Martins turned up with built-in hydraulic jacks in order to speed up pit stops, but their greatest asset was their driver line up: Stirling Moss/Roy Salvadori, Carroll Shelby/Jack Fairman and Maurice Trintignant/Paul Frere. At least Ferrari no longer relied upon the extraordinary side jacks of the last Nine Hours Race and their drivers were no less impressive: Tony Brooks/Dan Gurney, Olivier Gendebien/Giulio Cabianca and Phil Hill/Cliff Allison. They also brought a 2-litre Dino 196S for Giorgio Scarlatti/Lodovico Scarfiotti.

Favourites for the 2-litre class were the 1500cc Porsche RS60s for Wolfgang von Trips/Jo Bonnier, Umberto Maglioli/Edgar Barth and Hans Herrmann teamed with British guest Chris Bristow. In fact the German cars were fast enough at Goodwood to be an outside bet for outright victory. Nor could one rule out the home teams of Lotus, Lola and Elva. Even the sole Cooper, entered by John Coombs, was to be driven by the formidable combination of Jack Brabham and Bruce McLaren.

Stirling Moss's watch showed noon slightly in advance of the official starter's and he took off across the track while the starter still held the flag in the air. Some awaited the signal but most set off in pursuit of Moss who led the surge to Madgwick corner. Carroll Shelby's Aston was next, followed by Graham Hill's 2-litre Lotus 15, Graham Whitehead's private Aston Martin DBR1 and von Trips's Porsche. Gurney's Ferrari was stuck on the line for a short time and Phil Hill's car lasted only two laps – not a happy start for the Italian team, though Gurney wasted no time in moving through the field to third place.

The first batch of driver changes saw Salvadori in front of von Trips, Fairman, Trintignant, Tom Dickson's Lotus 15 and Cabianca's 2-litre Ferrari. This was a development of the car driven by Peter Collins at the 1958 Easter meeting and was left-hand drive, unlike the Testa Rossa Ferraris.

Despite their bolt-on wheels, Porsche were helped by slower tyre wear. David Piper's Lotus crashed at Madgwick when a tyre burst and, though taken to hospital, he was not seriously hurt.

At 2.35pm Salvadori brought the leading Aston Martin into the pits. In the excitement, fuel splashed onto the hot exhaust and Salvadori launched himself from the car to land head first on the grass, rolling over and over to extinguish the flames. This was largely successful but his right glove was still alight until smothered by a fast-thinking bystander using his cap. Salvadori's race was obviously run, as was the leading DBR1, which was pushed away covered in foam from the fast-acting circuit fire brigade. A bigger problem for Aston Martin was the state of their pit. The heat had buckled the scaffolding carrying the fuel storage tank, which had fallen onto the pit roof. In a most generous gesture, Graham Whitehead, who occupied the adjoining pit, withdrew his car and handed over his pit to the works team. 'Although I am not particularly athletic, I was out of the car like lightning with my overalls on fire', Salvadori said later.

The race now looked very different. Aston Martin's team manager was that perennial friend of Goodwood, Reg Parnell. He went into a huddle with Stirling Moss and the committee's verdict resulted in Jack Fairman being called in and Moss installed in the car. There followed one of those drives which marked out Moss from the rest.

At half distance the Porsche of von Trips and Bonnier had a considerable lead over the Aston Martin, but Moss was making up some two seconds a lap. Trintignant's Aston was third with Cliff Allison's Ferrari fourth, harried by Chris Bristow's Porsche. Half an hour later and Moss was in the lead. Allison handed over the Ferrari to Phil Hill, now in third place and pressing the Bonnier Porsche.

It seems that Jim Clark first became persuaded that he really had a future in front-line motor racing when he found himself able to match the speed of Masten Gregory in the ill-handling Tojeiro Jaguar. The pair were not to finish the race. Approaching Woodcote, Gregory found himself unable to slow. He had perfected his routine for such eventualities and as the earth bank loomed, he stood on the seat. On impact the car folded around the cockpit like a closing penknife. Meantime Masten was soaring skywards. He survived the accident with broken bones but in a lot better shape than the car.

Having tried just about every driver in each car, Ferrari's Tavoni and Chiti finally put Tony Brooks into the third place car. Von Trips was back in the Porsche and the leading players were now on stage for the final scene. If Ferrari could take second place they would draw with Aston Martin for the Championship, so Brooks simply had to catch von Trips and then go after Moss – that was all!

Jo Bonnier had put in a fine drive. Having handed over to von Trips, the Swedish driver ambled casually down to the chicane where he sat on the grass to watch the excitement of the closing laps. Moss blasted into the pits for his last scheduled stop to find a bandaged Roy Salvadori offering to drive the last stint. Stirling declined with thanks and set off almost two laps in the lead. He found himself between von Trips and Brooks on the road and it will come as no surprise that he did not make it difficult for Brooks to pass him to keep his pursuit of the Porsche alive. The gap between von Trips and Brooks had come down from 14 seconds to 4.5 seconds. The Ferrari pit hung out a signal to von Trips asking him politely to slow down. Bonnier, returned from his stroll, responded with a similar signal to Brooks. Needless to say, neither took any notice.

As six o'clock came, the chequered flag was held out and the Porsche was hammering down the straight with the Ferrari seemingly breathing down its neck. Von Trips flung the car around Woodcote, through the chicane and shot across the finishing line with the Ferrari unable to get ahead. Then came the crowd's hero, Stirling Moss, crossing the line almost a lap ahead to win his fourth Tourist Trophy and to capture the Championship for Aston Martin by two points from Ferrari, with Porsche just one point further back in third place.

This was to be the last of the classic sports car races. Aston Martin could be justly proud of their 100% record even though they had twice narrowly failed to burn the place down. The age of the true sports racing car was over. The grand touring car would take over in the short term and future sports racers would either be hybrids powered by large American engines, or modified single-seaters with sports bodies. The Nine Hours Races and Tourist Trophies had brought a golden age of sports car racing to the British public.

If saloon racing had caught on with the public then marque racing had proved a success with the drivers. The concept was simple. Draw up a list of eligible production sports cars, allow limited modifications and arrange a championship or two. One such was for the Freddie Dixon Trophy, won in 1959 by Chris Lawrence in his Morgan Plus Four. The Morgan's traditional silhouette had led MGAs, Triumph TRs, Austin Healey 100s and AC Aces. Many agreed that the Members' Meetings had been spoiled by the 'no spinning' rule, though it failed to stop Bill de Selincourt from completing a successful season by winning the *Motor Sport* Brooklands Memorial Trophy from Tony Maggs, both using Lotus Elevens though Maggs had the ex-Ecurie Ecosse Tojeiro Jaguar at the season's end. The final meeting was marred by the death in practice of John Townend, who crashed his Lotus Seven.

Lola Climax Mk 1

Eric Broadley's entry into motor racing came in 1956 with an 1172cc Ford-powered special for the 750 MC formula. The car was developed for 1957 and enjoyed a successful year driven by Eric and his cousin Graham. Thus encouraged, an 1100cc Climax-engined car was built which first appeared in mid-1958. A series of promising results was spoilt by a crash in a Goodwood members' meeting, followed by a hasty rebuild for the Tourist Trophy during which the car recorded the fastest lap by an 1100cc car. Three new cars were put in hand for 1959 and drivers Peter Ashdown, Peter Gammon, Michael Taylor and Allan Ross enjoyed a season during which the Lola dominated its class. It was visibly faster than its opposition due to its extremely light chassis and superior road-holding. The car continued in production until 1962 and was the car to beat until the rear-engined Lotus 23 set new standards at which to aim. Lola moved on to single-seaters and the Mk 6 GT, which became the basis of the Ford GT40, the mighty T70 and a whole host of designs for all classes of racing.

Lola Climax Mk 1s await their victorious appearance in the Easter small-capacity sports-car race, 30 March 1959.

Attention for
motorcyclist Ken
Kavanagh's Maserati
250F 2527. *(30/3/59
Author's collection)*

The Scuderia Centro
Sud Maserati 300S
3077 of Hernanos da
Silva Ramos. *(30/3/59
Author's collection)*

In a desperate search for a dry spot, Jack Brabham's Cooper Climax T49 has been wheeled to the middle of the muddy paddock next to Vic Derrington's accessory van. (*30/3/59 Author's collection*)

Lofty England, Roy Salvadori and John Coombs discuss the performance of the Jaguar 3.4 'BUY1', second in the Fordwater Trophy. (*30/3/59 Author's collection*)

Giorgio Scarlatti's
Maserati 250F 2523
retired from the Glover
Trophy F1 race.
*(30/3/59 Author's
collection)*

The Formula 2
Coopers of Jean
Lucienbonet (22),
Masten Gregory (23)
and Bruce McLaren
(24). *(30/3/59 Author's
collection)*

The Lotus Climax 15 606-1 of Michael Taylor with Doug Graham's sister car (615-2) adjacent. *(30/3/59 Author's collection)*

Not a Lotus in sight. The new Lola Mk 1s of Peter Ashdown, Peter Gammon and Michael Taylor with Tommy Dickson's Elva Mk 4 in fourth place on the grid. The Lolas finished in grid order. *(30/3/59)*

Peter Pilsworth in his
Riley 1.5 during the
saloon car race.
(25/4/59)

Winning its class in the
Whitsun Touring Car
Race is Jed Noble's
Austin A40. *(18/5/59)*

Ken Rudd's 'Rudd
Racing' AC Bristol,
driven by Jack Turner.
(18/5/59)

Eventual winner Ron
Flockhart in the Ecurie
Ecosse Tojeiro Jaguar
chases Jim Clark's
Border Reivers' Lister
Jaguar. *(18/5/59)*

Tourist Trophy pre-race fuelling for the Aston Martin DBR1/3 of Moss/Salvadori. *(5/9/59 Author's collection)*

Aston Martin DBR1/3 overseen by Reg Parnell as Salvadori prepares to take over from Moss. David Brown (sports jacket and dark trousers) watches from behind the car. *(5/9/59)*

The fire-damaged DBR1/3 is pushed away from the pits. Surprisingly the car ran first time after cleaning. *(5/9/59)*

The works Porsches of Hans Herrmann/Chris Bristow (24) and Jo Bonnier/Wolfgang von Trips (22). *(5/9/59 Author's collection)*

The Elva Climax Mk V
driven by McKee,
Brierley and Threlfall
to third in class.
*(5/9/59 Author's
collection)*

The winning Aston
Martin DBR1/2 at the
BP 'filling station'
before the start. *(5/9/59
Author's collection)*

Tony Brooks (1932–)

A 23-year-old dental student from Dukinfield in Cheshire won the 1955 Syracuse Grand Prix in a B-type Connaught, thus becoming the first British driver to win a continental Grand Prix in a British car since Sir Henry Segrave's victory at San Sebastian 31 years earlier. The win was the more remarkable since it was Tony Brooks's first race abroad and his first in an F1 car. Though incredible at the time, with hindsight it seems entirely reasonable that this feat should have been achieved by a driver of the consummate skill and intelligence of Tony Brooks. From racing the family Healey Silverstone in Goodwood club events, he progressed via Frazer Nash to the works Aston Martin team, where he shared a car in the ill-fated 1955 Le Mans with John Riseley-Pritchard. Under pressure from his family, Riseley-Pritchard retired from racing after the Le Mans disaster and he

invited Brooks to drive his F2 Connaught in several events, this leading to his invitation to the works team and Syracuse. BRM snapped him up for 1956 but it was an unhappy experience, particularly when the car tipped him out and caught fire at Silverstone. 1957 saw him join the Vanwall team and, despite serious injuries from a crash at Le Mans, he shared the first place with Moss in the British GP at Aintree. He won the Nurburgring 1,000km and Spa 1,000km for Aston Martin. In 1958 he won the Belgian, Italian and German GPs for Vanwall and shared the TT win with Moss. Moving to Ferrari in 1959, he won the French and German GPs, finishing second in the world championship. He drove for Yeoman Credit Cooper in 1960 and for BRM in 1961, but family ties and his Weybridge garage business took precedence and he retired at the top of his considerable form. The smoothness of his style on circuits such as Spa and the Nurburgring will never be forgotten

Tony Brooks took the Easter 1957 F2 race in Rob Walker's earlier T41 Cooper in the face of newer works entries.

1960

1960 and a new decade began, but Goodwood also looked back with the presentation by journalist Tommy Wisdom of the Brooklands paddock gates. They were renovated and placed at the entrance to the marshalling area. A sign reminded the modern generation that every driver racing at Brooklands from 1907 to 1939 had passed through these portals.

Jack Brabham had won the world championship with Cooper and motor racing would never be the same again. Only Ferrari among Formula 1 constructors retained a front-engined layout. Formula Three (500cc) was in decline, but a new international formula was spawned in Italy for 1100cc production-engined single-seaters – Formula Junior. Fifteen of the new cars lined up for the first race of the 1960 Easter meeting. Lotus now had the engine behind the driver and the driver was Jim Clark. The new Lotus Eighteen came in various guises; with 997cc Ford power for Formula Junior, 1500cc Climax power for Formula 2 and 2500cc Climax for Formula 1. That it won all three races suggested that Mr Chapman had found his first really successful single-seater design.

That Jim Clark should win the Formula Junior event from team mate Trevor Taylor was perhaps predictable in view of his performance at the preceding Members' Meeting in March. In his first outing with a works Lotus he had found himself up against a man in his first motor race. This was not only the first car race in which John Surtees had competed, but also the first which he had attended. Ken Tyrrell provided him with a Cooper BMC in which to gain the experience needed for his international licence. Clark and Surtees engaged in their own race, leaving the opposition behind. They swapped the lead repeatedly and the infighting allowed Trevor Taylor to reel them in and join the fun, but it was Clark who won with Surtees second. Sixth came another young man in his first single-seater race – Mike Spence.

So Jim Clark came to the Easter meeting having already won Goodwood's first event for the new formula and he repeated his victory, this time with only teammate Taylor to beat. Third was Mike McKee in Jim Russell's Lotus 18, with Henry Taylor fourth in one of Ken Tyrrell's three Cooper BMC T52s.

There were not enough F2 Lotus 18s available to give Clark a drive in the Lavant Cup but team leader Innes Ireland took the only available chassis to victory ahead of Stirling Moss in the F2 single-seat Porsche 718. Porsche had turned up at the Tourist Trophy the previous September with an F2 car in the transporter. Moss had tried it and Rob Walker arranged to enter an example for the 1960 season. The Yeoman Credit finance company had decided to go racing in a grand manner and produced smart apple green and red Coopers for both F2 and F1, to be driven by Harry Schell and Chris Bristow. Among the Formula 2 entries was a visitor from New Zealand, Denny Hulme.

The Sussex Trophy for sports cars (note that there was only one race for sports cars of any engine size) was notable for the total absence of works cars. Aston Martin, Jaguar and Lister had all withdrawn from active competition though their cars soldiered on in private teams. Even the Aston Martin DBR1 which had caught fire at the Tourist Trophy was back, now with Border Reivers and driven by Jim Clark. In fact, despite its appearance, it had been found that the car was still drivable immediately after its fiery mishap.

Since Reg Parnell's retirement as a driver, Roy Salvadori had taken over as the circuit's most regular winner. More success came at the wheel of John Coombs's Cooper Monaco with full 2½-litre Climax power. Jim Clark was making a race of it when the Aston Martin DBR1 cried enough after five laps. Second place fell to Jimmy Blumer's 2-litre Cooper Monaco and Tom Dickson's Lotus Fifteen came home third. The Jaguar D engine had been extended to 3.8 litres, but not even this enabled the Listers and D-types to keep up with the smaller-engined Cooper and Lotus.

The Glover Trophy F1 race saw the British debut of the rear-engined BRM T48 driven by Graham Hill and Dan Gurney, while Jo Bonnier elected to give the front-engined T25 its swansong. Lotus provided two examples of the senior member of the Eighteen family for Innes Ireland and Alan Stacey. Jack Brabham was away winning the F2 race at Pau in southern France. The two meetings often clashed, diluting the entry at both. Cooper sent one car to Goodwood for Bruce McLaren but it was the new Yeoman Credit racing team Cooper Climax T51 of Chris Bristow that claimed pole position. The finance company joined with British Racing Partnership run by Stirling Moss's father Alfred and manager Ken Gregory to run a fleet of immaculate Coopers in F1 and F2. Bristow's team mate was Franco-American Harry Schell. Harry was one of motor racing's true characters, not beyond signing his autograph 'Shell', just to hint at a link with a certain oil company.

Tony Vandervell had not regained his health but could not keep away from motor racing. In a much-reduced effort, his team had pared down one of the

1958 Vanwalls (VW5) to produce a lightened, smoother vehicle for Tony Brooks to drive when he was not engaged with Ferrari. It was significant that even Brooks could only manage seventh fastest practice time.

Gilby Engineering bought the Cooper Maserati that Roy Salvadori drove in 1959. Sid Greene's son Keith was the driver. Tommy Atkins now had one of the previous year's works Cooper Climax T51s for Roy Salvadori.

The Cooper works were developing the 'lowline' T53 in direct response to the performance of the Lotus 18, but Rob Walker's T51 was second on the grid with Stirling Moss at the wheel. Harry Schell was third and Innes Ireland's Lotus fourth. Bristow led from the start but Moss was soon in front – but not for long. Ireland shattered the lap record at 101.17 mph and from then on held off every assault from the Walker Cooper. The speed mounted and the race ended with an average speed of 100.39mph. Fastest lap fell to Ireland at 102.13mph. He and Moss both took home one of the BARC's new trophies, the Goodwood Ton, awarded for a lap in excess of 100mph. The newspapers made much of Moss being beaten twice on one day, the headlines being reminiscent of those that had followed Hawthorn's success eight years earlier.

Lotus were ecstatic at their first F1 win. BRM were less content - their cars were lapped, and the Vanwall finished last. 'We brought out the first rear-engined BRM – and what a pig it was!', commented Graham Hill.

The final race of the day was for 'closed cars'. This admitted Equipe Endeavour's Aston Martin DB4GT for Stirling Moss to drive to victory some 22 seconds ahead of Roy Salvadori in John Coombs's Jaguar 3.8. By the end of the season the Aston Martin would be firmly in the GT class, as would the Lotus Elites of Peter Lumsden and Jonathan Williams, which finished first and second in their class. The Speedwell Team's Austin Healey Sprite should have been driven by John Venner Pack, but he had been injured in the Formula Junior race. Len Adams was called to the circuit to replace him and arrived in time to win his class.

Ecurie Ecosse again took the main prize at the Whitsun meeting, Tom Dickson driving their Cooper Monaco to beat off the Lotus Fifteens of Doug Graham and Chris Martyn.

The RAC had been advised that the club could not organise another Tourist Trophy, but they were persuaded to add a three-hour GT race to their proposed Formula Junior Championship meeting on 20 August. The programme consisted of two seven-lap FJ heats and a 21-lap final, followed by a three-hour Tourist Trophy for GT cars.

Formula Junior had grown in popularity during its first UK season and a huge field was gathered for the BARC's championship race. Team Lotus entered three cars, Peter Arundell and Trevor Taylor in the first heat and Jim Clark in the second. Ken Tyrrell's quasi-works Coopers were to be handled by

John Love and John Surtees, but the latter non-started. The Lotus 18 and the Ford engine had proved the most successful combination but there was a rich variety on offer with cars from Cooper, Lola, Elva, Gemini, Envoy, Alexis, Deep Sanderson, Scorpion, Terrier, Venom and Yimkin. The formula was intended as a nursery for the higher echelons of the sport. The works Lotus drivers would all make the grade, as would John Love, Mike Spence, Alan Rees, Tony Maggs, Frank Gardner, Tim Parnell, Hugh Dibley and John Fenning, all among the day's entry.

The first heat fell to Trevor Taylor's Lotus from Dick Prior's Lola and Cliff Johnson's Lotus. The second heat was won, almost inevitably, by Jim Clark, though Mike McKee had claimed pole position and finished second. Peter Ashdown's Lola was third. The first 12 from each heat combined for the 21-lap final. Trevor Taylor had been quickest in his heat and took pole position. Against expectations he also won the final despite all that Jim Clark could throw at him. Third was Mike McKee with the Lolas of Dennis Taylor and Peter Ashdown next and John Hine's Lotus sixth.

Stirling Moss had persuaded Rob Walker to add a Lotus 18 to the équipe, but it had bitten him at the Belgian Grand Prix in Spa. Moss had been badly hurt but was soon back in the saddle though not completely fit by the time that Rob Walker and Dick Wilkins got together to provide him with a Ferrari 250GT SWB (short wheelbase) for the Tourist Trophy. Graham Whitehead had a similar model to share with Jack Fairman as did Wolfgang Seidel and Willy Mairesse. The older 250GTs were entered by Scuderia Serenissima for Colin Davis (now racing mostly in Italy), Jo Schlesser and Pierre 'Loustel' Dumay. John Ogier entered two Aston Martin DB4GTs for Roy Salvadori and Innes Ireland/John Whitmore. The large capacity class was completed by two Austin Healey 3000s for Peter Riley and John Bekaert.

The 2-litre class boasted four Porsche 1600GS models, two works cars for Graham Hill and Jo Bonnier and two private entries for Gerhard Koch and Fritz Hahnl. Dickie Stoop in his own Porsche 356 was faster in practice than Hahnl. Dick Jacobs's MGA Twin Cams were beautifully prepared as always and not out of their depth in such exotic company, due in no small measure to the skill of their drivers, Tommy Bridger and Alan Foster. Also no slowcoach was Chris Lawrence in the Morgan, though the three Elva Couriers and the supercharged Austin Healey Sprite were struggling.

The third class consisted of eleven Lotus Elites, many of which were faster than the 2-litre runners. Quickest were Mike Parkes/Sir Gawaine Baillie, Tom Dickson and Chris Summers.

If Stirling Moss's driving had not been slowed by his accident, his sprinting was not yet up to standard. Though not the first to reach his car, he was the first to complete the opening lap with Salvadori, Loustel, Schlesser and

Whitehead in his wake. It took only four laps before the back markers began to be lapped, indicating the considerable speed differential. Ireland brought the second Aston Martin through the massed ranks of Ferraris into third place. Salvadori took the lead from Moss for a couple of laps. After 45 minutes the leading cars began their pit stops. Then Salvadori had a tyre explode at Lavant corner and the time taken to tour round to the pits effectively ended his challenge for the lead. Both Dickson's Lotus Elite and Loustel's Ferrari ended in the bank at Woodcote corner in separate incidents.

After two hours the order was Moss, Ireland, Salvadori, Davis, and Hill in the leading Porsche. Parkes was the leading Elite driver. It seemed that Aston Martin's sports car record was not to be equalled by their GT cars when Ireland came into the pits, exhaust dragging on the road. This dropped both Astons a lap behind Moss who drove to a comfortable win without relaxing his concentration or his speed.

Graham Hill won the 2-litre class and Parkes should have won the 1500cc class. He had the miserable luck to burst a tyre at Lavant corner right at the end of the race. His ensuing visit to the scenery collected a length of fencing wire which wound around the wheel spokes. He shed the tyre on his way to the pits but the mechanics had to disentangle the wire before they could fit a new wheel. Meanwhile, the new class leader John Lumsden was fighting wheel-to-wheel with Graham Warner. The two collided at the chicane, Warner dropping behind to see Lumsden take the flag at six o'clock. Moss had just passed by and had to complete another lap before he could claim his sixth Tourist Trophy.

The final Members' Meeting closed with a race for journalists and commentators, all driving factory-provided Minis. The victor was Ronald 'Steady' Barker of *The Autocar* followed by Roger Bell (*Motor*), John Anstice Brown (*Motor*) and John Bolster (*Autosport*). The first Minis were starting to appear in motor sport and this publicity exercise did BMC no harm. As both James Tilling and Anthony Marsh were driving, the microphones were taken over by Tony Brooks and Les Leston. They were sure that they were rather better at commentating than the commentators were at driving.

On pole is van Sickle's Lotus 11 with Brierley's Elva Mk V next to him. No.4 is de Waldkirch's Lotus 17 and No.3 Cliff Dade's Lotus 11. *(19/3/60)*

Before digital electronic readouts cars were weighed on a Salter spring balance. Peter Ashdown's Elva DKW 100 would appear to tip the scales at 1009 pounds. *(19/3/60)*

Leslie Fagg's Deep Sanderson Ford Formula Junior on the grid next to Clive Puzey's Yimkin BMC. *(19/3/60)*

John Surtees not only drove in the first car race that he ever attended but finished second to Jim Clark's Lotus. Here he is in Ken Tyrrell's Formula Junior Cooper BMC. *(19/3/60)*

The Yeoman Credit
Cooper T51 driven
by Harry Schell.
(18/4/60)

Graham Whitehead in his Lister Jaguar (BHL103) on his way to fifth place in the Sussex Trophy. *(18/4/60)*

Le Mans start for the Sussex Trophy: Roy Salvadori Cooper Monaco (83), Tom Dickson Lotus 15 (88), Jimmy Blumer Cooper Monaco (85), Jim Clark Aston Martin DBR1/3 (76), Michael Taylor Lotus 15 (86) and Graham Whitehead Lister Jaguar (72). *(18/4/60)*

Brian Hart drives Len Terry's Terrier Ford Mk 4 Formula Junior car. *(18/4/60)*

Cars gathered in the assembly area include Jimmy Saunders' Victoria Climax (37). *(7/5/60)*

Members' Meeting sports car race for Ken Lyon Lotus 11 (27), Rudi de Waldkirch Lotus 17 (24), Brian Gubby Lotus 11 (21), Kathleen Howard Lotus 11 (26) and J.G. Bloore Elva Mk 4 (33). *(7/5/60)*

Start scene includes James van Sickle Lotus 11 (30), Peter Boshier Jones Lotus 11 (34), Bill Pinckney Lotus 11 (27) and Tim Horton Lotus 17 (22). *(25/6/60)*

Formula Junior
Championship heat
two: Mike McKee
Lotus 18 (10), John
Hine Lotus 18 (16) and
Jim Clark Lotus 18 (6).
(20/8/60)

The Ferrari 250GT SWB chassis 2119 of Stirling Moss, which added yet another Tourist Trophy victory to his impressive record. *(20/8/60)*

Through the chicane goes the Wolfgang Seidel/Willy Mairesse Ferrari 250GT 1807, chased by winner Stirling Moss. *(20/8/60)*

'Bad news Herr Bonnier. The engine is stolen.' Von Hanstein checks the wrong end during the Porsche's pit stop. *(20/8/60)*

Lotus Climax 18

The first Lotus single-seaters, the 12 and 16, had not stood up well against their Cooper rivals. Colin Chapman's next design, the 18, was to be a very different beast. Affectionately known as the biscuit tin, the most important innovation was siting the engine behind the driver. The car came in FJ, F2 and F1 variants and was hugely successful in all forms. Having gazed at the back of Innes Ireland's cars in F1 and F2 races at the Easter Goodwood, Stirling Moss prevailed on patron Rob Walker to provide him with an 18 and in this car he won Lotus their first GP (Monaco) also taking the US event at Riverside. This was despite a hub failure that tipped him into an almighty crash at Spa and caused injuries that kept him out of racing for many weeks. The Walker team was forced to continue with the 18, contractual complications preventing Chapman from selling them the next generation 21. Despite this, Moss won at Monaco and the Nurburgring in two of his finest drives. The 18 continued as a willing workhorse for numerous private F1, F2 and FJ teams and it was in a much-modified 18 with V8 Climax power that Stirling Moss was to end his front-line career against the bank at Goodwood's St Mary's Corner in 1962.

Twice in a day Innes Ireland kept a Lotus 18 ahead of Stirling Moss. Here he wins the Glover Trophy to give Lotus its first F1 victory, 18 April 1960.

Chris Bristow (1937–1960)

From 1956 when he began racing with a Leonard MG to his untimely death in 1960, Chris Bristow's progress could be described as meteoric in all senses.

With his father's backing he moved from the Leonard to a Cooper Climax T39 in 1956 and a place in the Elva team for 1958. John Hume provided drives in his 1460cc Lotus 11 and, later, his modified Cooper F2 car. 1959 saw him drive the Moorland Climax and a Cooper Monaco. His reward came in 1959 with F2 drives for BRP and a guest seat in a Porsche at the TT. BRP joined with Yeoman Credit for 1960 and Bristow joined Harry Schell in a fully funded GP team, running specially built Cooper T51s in both F1 and F2 events. When Schell was killed at Silverstone, Bristow found himself team leader. Whether this put him under extra pressure we shall never know, but he crashed during the Belgian GP at Spa and was killed instantly. From the beginning of his career he was always blindingly fast. There were those pundits who said that he was destined for greatness and those who said that he would inevitably end in disaster.

Chris Bristow is visibly quicker than Harry Schell in the sister car and photographed at the same corner (see p169).

1961

FOR 1961 the BARC organised races not only at Goodwood, Aintree and Crystal Palace but also at Mallory Park and Oulton Park. This demanding programme did not deter them from putting on eight meetings at Goodwood. The Members' Meetings usually included Formula Junior as well as sports and saloons. There was now a considerable choice for the amateur racer with both new and second-hand competition cars readily available. The sport had come a long way in the 12 years since the circuit had opened.

Much to the disgust of the British constructors, Formula 1 had been changed to an engine limit of 1500cc. In an effort to extend the life of existing F1 cars and in the hope of tempting the Americans to join in, the Intercontinental Formula had been dreamed up. An upper engine limit of 3 litres did at least bring Reventlow's Scarab over from the States for the fearless Chuck Daigh to drive against an assortment of 1960 F1 cars in the formula's first race at the Easter Goodwood meeting. BRM entered two P48s for Graham Hill and new recruit Tony Brooks. Stirling Moss had a choice of Cooper or Lotus but chose the former. Yeoman Credit continued racing despite the deaths of both their previous drivers, Chris Bristow and Harry Schell, in separate accidents during 1960. They were replaced by Roy Salvadori and John Surtees. Bruce McLaren drove a Cooper for Tommy Atkins and came home second to Moss with Hill's BRM third.

The meeting had started in pouring rain with the St Mary's Trophy for saloons won by Mike Parkes from Graham Hill, both in Tommy Sopwith's Equipe Endeavour 3.8 Jaguars. Quickest of the Minis was John Whitmore. In these days before John Cooper worked his magic on the little car, Whitmore's standard Mini was prepared by Don Moore. The 2-litre class fell to another saloon-racing legend, Bill Blydenstein in his Borgward Isabella.

Enzo Ferrari famously scorned the British racing car manufacturers as '*garagistes*' who bolted together bits and pieces of other people's products. Only Ferrari and BRM built their own engines and now even BRM were relying on the ubiquitous Coventry Climax engine while awaiting the development of their own 1500cc unit for the new Formula 1. For the first time in many years there were no works Coopers entered for the Glover Trophy 100-mile race. There were two T53s for Yeoman Credit drivers Roy Salvadori and John Surtees. Rival finance company United Dominions Trust, partnered by Laystall Engineering and the British Racing Partnership, entered two Lotus 18s for Cliff Allison and Henry Taylor. Team Lotus had a single 18 for Innes Ireland and Rob Walker another for Stirling Moss. The Climax-engined BRM P48/57s were to be driven by Graham Hill and Tony Brooks. Gilby Engineering had built their own F1 car designed by Len Terry for Keith Greene to drive. Another newcomer was the works Emeryson driven by Bruce Halford.

Though Moss was fastest in practice it was Surtees that led from start to finish. Moss chased him hard until his engine faltered and, 10 laps from the finish, both Hill and Salvadori passed him. Ireland brought the works Lotus home fifth with Henry Taylor sixth.

Yeoman Credit would have been well satisfied with first and third and so it was fitting that the other finance company should take revenge in the sports car race. Colin Chapman had introduced his rear-engined Nineteen, nicknamed 'Monte Carlo' in retaliation for the Cooper T49 'Monaco'. UDT Laystall brought three cars to Goodwood for Stirling Moss, Cliff Allison and Henry Taylor. Despite the presence of privately entered Aston Martin DBR2s, DBR1s, numerous D-type Jaguars, Lister Jaguars and others, the Nineteens took first and second for Moss and Taylor, Allison being delayed at the start. The smaller class fell to John Bekaert's Lola Mk 1, the entire field for this class being only three of these machines.

The Fordwater Trophy for GT cars included Stirling Moss in a new Aston Martin DB4GT Zagato entered by Rob Walker but, in a rather thin field, it was Mike Parkes who won in a Ferrari 250GT SWB entered jointly by Tommy Sopwith's Equipe Endeavour and Colonel Ronnie Hoare's Maranello Concessionaires. This was the new team's second race and second win. This was not just any Ferrari but the car in which Moss had won the 1960 Tourist Trophy at Goodwood. Two of the new E-type Jaguars had been entered but both non-started.

The most exciting race of the day was the 10-lap Chichester Cup for Formula Junior cars. Fastest in practice had been Jim Russell, who had Tony Maggs, Dan Collins and Dick Prior beside him on the grid. As the flag fell Peter Arundell surged through from the second row, but was nudged from behind, catching Maggs and pushing him into Russell, Mike McKee also joining in the accident. Russell lost a wheel, which bounded towards Alan Rees, who slammed on his brakes and was hit by Mike Parkes whose Gemini ended up on top of Alan Rees's Lotus. Russell (who was making a comeback after two years away from racing following a serious accident at Le Mans) was left facing the wrong way in his newly converted Lotus tricycle while the rest of the field hurtled towards him, mostly swerving aside at the last moment though the odd car glanced off him. Meanwhile the field was diving in all directions, many of these avoidance efforts resulting in other minor collisions. Dan Collins had got away in advance of the fracas and led into Woodcote – but not out of it, having charged the bank in his glee at having dodged the carnage. Dick Prior and John Hine found themselves leading in their Lolas with Tony Maggs (Tyrrell Cooper) third and a surprised Brian Hart fourth in the front-engined Terrier.

The Lolas then eliminated each other when Prior spun at the chicane and was hit by Hine. Tony Maggs and Brian Hart picked their way slowly through the wreckage. Peter Arundell was delayed by the start-line excitement and spent the race hurling his works Lotus 20 through the field and avoiding other people's accidents. He picked off Hart and went after the leader to such good effect that the two spent much of the final lap side-by-side. Arundell seemed to have the edge leaving the chicane but Maggs found enough steam to get back alongside as they crossed the finish line. For the first and only time at Goodwood a dead heat was declared.

The Whitsun meeting was marred by the death of Roy Bloxam, who crashed his ex-works Lister Jaguar in the last race of the day. Ecurie Ecosse won the feature sports car race yet again, Bruce Halford behind the wheel of their Cooper Monaco. The pre-war racing car handicap fell to the Hon. Patrick Lindsay's ERA R5B.

The Tourist Trophy meeting again featured the Formula Junior championship and the TT itself, again for GT cars. Jack Brabham's first creation, the MRD Ford, was driven in the first heat by New Zealander Gavin Youl. Fastest in practice, he led until a little over-enthusiasm slipped him back to fourth. Frank Gardner took over the lead in his Lotus 20, entered by the Jim Russell Racing Drivers' School, and fended off John Rhodes's Cooper BMC T56. Third was Bill Moss in the works Gemini Mk 3a.

The second heat fell to Alan Rees in his Lotus 20, who also avoided a first lap multiple pile-up to win the final ahead of Youl's MRD and Dennis Taylor's Lola Mk 3.

The three-hour Tourist Trophy boasted two works Porsche 695GS Abarths for Graham Hill and Hubert Linge and similar cars for Gerhard Koch and Fritz Hahnl. John Ogier brought three Aston Martins, two DB4GT Zagatos for Roy Salvadori and Jim Clark and a DB4GT for Innes Ireland. The favourites had to be Mike Parkes in the Equipe Endeavour/Maranello Concessionaires Ferrari

250GT SWB and the similar Rob Walker car for six times TT winner Stirling Moss.

In addition to the Porsches (and in stark contrast to the German cars' sleek Abarth-designed bodies) the 2-litre class included three works supported Morgan +4s for Chris Lawrence, Peter Marten and Richard Shepherd-Barron. The smaller class contained only Lotus Elites, including the famous Graham Warner car ('LOV1') and Les Leston's 'DAD10'.

Parkes was marginally quicker in practice and led from the Le Mans start with the Clark and Salvadori Astons and Moss following. Moss was second by the end of the first lap and closed on Parkes. Salvadori passed Clark and Ireland disentangled himself from the Porsches so that the two Ferraris and three Aston Martins were now in line astern. The season-long battle between the Warner and Leston Elites was continued until Warner was forced to retire.

Jim Clark was called in to the pits for the boot lid of his Aston Martin to be closed. Tyre wear was to prove decisive. Only 17 laps into the race the pit stops began, with Parkes calling for four new tyres. Moss kept the lead through his own pit stop, when only the rear wheels were replaced. Parkes was charging hard in his pursuit of Moss and needed to change all four wheels after 37 laps, the stop dropping him to fourth. 'Not only were we using tyres at a faster rate than the Ferraris (I changed 14 tyres) but our pit stops were slower', said Roy Salvadori.

American Allen Markelson's Chevrolet Corvette was struggling on worn tyres, the spares being held up at the airport. His misery increased when the car started to belch clouds of smoke and steam. He was black flagged when the car started to lose its oil. Also black flagged was Parkes, who had damaged the Ferrari's undertray when he took to the grass. This cost him time in the pits for repairs and at half distance Moss led from Salvadori and Ireland. Graham Hill led the 2-litre class by two laps from Hahnl, while Leston and Lumsden headed the 1300cc class.

Parkes was second once again though Salvadori was chasing hard. Moss was comfortable at the front and consuming tyres at a slower rate than his rivals. Lumsden broke the class record several times in his pursuit of Leston, who reached 128mph on the straight.

Moss finished a lap ahead of the field to win his seventh Tourist Trophy, listening, so we were told, to the BBC race commentary on his car radio.

The season-long battle for the *Motor Sport* Brooklands Memorial Trophy ended in a three-way tie between Jon Derisley, remarkably fast in his Lotus Seven, Laurie Keens, consistently successful in his Lola Mk 1, and Geoff Oliver, Derisley's rival, driving his DRW Ford.

Graham Hill in Tommy Sopwith's Equipe Endeavour Jaguar 3.8, second to Mike Parkes in the St Marys' Trophy. *(3/4/61)*

The Yeoman Credit Racing Team with John Surtees's Intercontinental Cooper Climax T53 F1-5-61 in the foreground. *(3/4/61 Author's collection)*

Graham Hill in the
Climax-engined BRM
P48/571. *(3/4/61
Author's collection)*

Jim Clark in John
Ogier's Aston Martin
DB4GT Zagato
finished fourth in the
Tourist Trophy.
(19/8/61)

Allen Markelson retired his battered Chevrolet Corvette from the Tourist Trophy after 42 laps. *(19/8/61)*

Porsche line up for the Tourist Trophy with the 695GS cars of Hubert Linge (21), Graham Hill (20), Fritz Hahnl (23) and Gerhard Koch (22). *(19/8/61)*

Mike Parkes, fastest in practice and second in the Tourist Trophy with the Ferrari 250 GT 2417 entered jointly by Equipe Endeavour and Maranello Concessionaires. *(19/8/61)*

Scarab

Lance Reventlow, Woolworths heir and American sports-racing fan, built his own Scarab cars having decided that the standards of the European constructors were pretty low. He employed the best brains available and produced a well-proportioned car built to a high standard, which swept the board in US racing in 1958. The cars were then sold and Reventlow turned to his F1 project, which was as complicated as the sports car had been simple. A space frame chassis was to carry an engine owing much to Mercedes-Benz design, with desmodromic valve gear and twin-camshafts. The car inevitably took longer than anticipated to build and did not appear until 1959, by which time its front-engined layout was out of date. A similar fate befell the Aston Martin GP project and no amount of development could make up for such a major change in design concept. Two cars came to Europe for Reventlow and Chuck Daigh to drive but, by mid-season, they knew they were wasting their time and went back to the US. In 1960 one car came back to Europe for Daigh to drive in the ill-fated Intercontinental series. Running with a 3-litre engine it was still no match for its rear-engined opponents – an interesting car but born too late.

Fitted with a 3-litre engine, the former GP Scarab had a brief second career in Intercontinental Formula events, as here at Goodwood on 3 April 1961.

Bruce McLaren, one of the safest drivers of his generation, killed in a tragic testing accident at Goodwood.

Bruce McLaren (1937–1970)

Born in New Zealand, Bruce McLaren came to Europe in 1958. He was sponsored by the New Zealand Grand Prix Association and, endorsed by Jack Brabham, it was no surprise that he found a home in the Cooper team. After a good year in F2 he was promoted to the GP team alongside Brabham. By the end of the year he had become the youngest Grand Prix winner by taking the US event at Sebring. He followed this with a win in Argentina at the start of the next season and shadowed team-leader Brabham as Jack won his second championship. When Brabham left Coopers to build his own cars, Bruce was new team leader, but the team's fortunes were in decline. In 1964 he formed his own team to race during the winter 'down under' and out of Bruce McLaren Motor Racing came one of motor racing's all-time greats. The first McLaren F1 car appeared in 1966 and he and Denny Hulme were seen at the front of F1 and were unbeatable in CanAm.

Bruce McLaren was acknowledged as the safest driver of his era. It was particularly cruel that he should die in a testing accident at Goodwood in 1970.

1962

A BUSY WINTER at the circuit saw a major resurfacing of the track. Some 2,000 tons of asphalt created a new surface three-quarters of an inch thick over 50,000 square yards, with flush concrete kerbings. Over £10,000 was spent.

The Easter meeting was to prove an unwelcome landmark in British motor racing. Ferrari had dominated the first year of the 1½-litre Formula 1 and the British constructors were relieved by the introduction of the Coventry Climax V8 engine. BRM also now had their own V8 in the back of the P57 with drivers Graham Hill and Richie Ginther. Only two of the new Climax units made it to Goodwood, one in John Surtees's Bowmaker Yeoman Lola Mk 4 (Eric Broadley's first F1 car) and the other in Rob Walker's Lotus for Stirling Moss.

The Walker car was a Lotus 18, updated to Lotus 21 specification and modified to take the new engine. It had been suggested that Moss should race at Pau. Motor racing was truly international and the opportunities for top-flight drivers to race in the UK were diminishing. Moss was keen to race before his home crowd and opted for Goodwood. The car had been prepared for earlier races by the UDT team and was painted in their pale green colours. They offered to return it to Rob Walker's dark blue racing colours but, as UDT were preparing the car, it was decided it should remain green.

Moss pipped Graham Hill for pole position with Bruce McLaren's works Cooper T55 sharing the front row. Innes Ireland's UDT Lotus 18/21 and Surtees's Lola made up the second row with Ginther (BRM), Tony Shelly (Lotus 18/21) and Masten Gregory (UDT Lotus 18/21) behind them.

McLaren in the 1961 Cooper was quickest off the mark, followed by Hill, Moss, Ireland, Surtees and Gregory. He said later 'I made a tremendous start and, for two glorious laps, led all the F1 cars with the old four-cylinder Cooper'. The second BRM was left on the grid, Ginther losing two laps before getting away. Meanwhile his teammate Hill pushed the BRM with its upswept 'rocket launcher' exhaust into the lead. Ireland demoted Moss a place before Surtees passed both of them. McLaren held on to Hill until they came upon Ginther, Hill passing quickly but McLaren taking some time to find a way through. This allowed Hill to build a lead that he never lost.

Moss stopped at his pit on lap nine, losing a lap while mechanics attended to a gearbox problem. With no chance of winning, Moss seemed to be driving faster than ever, perhaps with an eye to the lap record, which he duly captured at 105.37mph, though Surtees equalled the time.

Hill was well ahead of McLaren when Moss, in seventh place, caught up with him entering St Mary's. A marshal showed Hill the blue flag to indicate that a faster car was behind him. Moss moved to pass on the left and then took to the grass, going straight on where the road bends right and drops away. Whether Moss moved left thinking that Hill might pull across him or perhaps his throttle stuck open we shall never know. The Lotus hit the earth bank head-on at about 60mph and disintegrated around the driver. It took some 40 minutes to extricate the hapless Moss. Broken limbs were the least of his injuries.

Much more worrying were the severe head wounds that resulted in bruising to the right side of the brain. We now know that, after a month in a coma and six months with paralysis down his left side, Moss made a full recovery, surviving to become the eternal symbol of British motor racing. At the time the crowd was hushed in disbelief that our greatest driver could be gravely injured.

The race ran its course, with Graham Hill winning at the start of what would be his first championship-winning year and the culmination of so much effort on the part of the BRM team. But there was little rejoicing. Even the weather joined in the mood with rain falling for the last race in which Moss should have raced the new Ferrari 250GTO for the first time. It was left to Mike Parkes in the rival Endeavour/Maranello car to debut this landmark car in the UK, though he was beaten in the race by Innes Ireland in the UDT Lotus 19.

Peter Arundell maintained Lotus success in the Formula Junior race while Bruce McLaren won the Lavant Cup 21-lap race for four-cylinder F1 cars. The St Mary's Trophy saloon race was a Jaguar benefit as usual with a second win of the day for Graham Hill from Roy Salvadori. The new works team of Mini Coopers all retired when their Dunlop SP tyres threw their treads. The class fell to Christabel Carlisle's Don Moore-entered Austin Mini Cooper.

The daily papers were filled with details of the Moss crash, including graphic illustrations of its immediate aftermath. His slow recovery received nearly as much attention until, a year later, he tried a few laps back at Goodwood in a UDT Lotus 19. It was not that his speed had diminished but that he felt his automatic responses had faded that persuaded him, perhaps prematurely, to retire from active racing.

The Whitsun Trophy was won by Jimmy Blumer's Cooper Monaco after 'Dizzy' Addicott's fearsome Buick-engined Lotus 15 had retired. There were no works entries and even the Ecurie Ecosse cars non-started.

Veedol Oil had sponsored a championship for young drivers in production sports cars and the final was to be the opening race of the Tourist Trophy meeting. David Cole won the race in his Lotus 7, but Bob Burnard and his AC Bristol took the championship and with it the first prize, a Lotus 20 Formula Junior car.

The Formula Junior championship was restricted to a single race of 21 laps, with the Team Lotus entries, Peter Arundell, Alan Rees and ex-motorcyclist Bob Anderson starting as favourites. Arundell was never headed and missed a 100mph lap by a whisker, more than the outright circuit record just three years earlier. Alan Rees dropped back from second place with a failing gearbox to be replaced by Mike Spence (Lotus) who then suffered the same malady. Frank Gardner fell out when his exhaust collapsed, leaving Richard Attwood's Cooper T59 in second place with Bob Anderson third.

The Tourist Trophy itself was to be run over 100 laps. As this would take about two and a half hours it was actually a reduction from the previous three-hour race. From its debut at the Easter meeting, the Ferrari 250GTO had become the GT car to beat. The Endeavour/Maranello car driven by Mike Parkes had a very successful season. Maranello Concessionaires had also joined with Bowmaker to run a second car for John Surtees. David Piper had been one of the first private owners to take delivery of a GTO, UDT had one for Innes Ireland and John Coombs another for Graham Hill. Coombs's team also fielded an E-type Jaguar for Roy Salvadori as did Peter Lumsden and Dick Protheroe. John Ogier's Aston Martin DB4GT Zagatos were piloted by Jim Clark and Graham Warner, while Mike Salmon drove his privately owned example. The large-engined class was completed by Dan Collins' Chevrolet Corvette.

There were no works Porsches in 1962, but Ben Pon brought his 695GS over from Holland. There was a host of Lotus Elites, three works-supported Morgans, three Sunbeam Alpines entered by Alan Fraser, three works TVRs and a Sprite.

Ireland was quickest in practice followed by Surtees, Parkes and Hill. Clark was fastest of the Aston Martins and first away at the Le Mans start, though he was overwhelmed by Ferrari power before the first lap was over. Parkes was delayed at the start and carved his way through the pack to third place behind Surtees and Ireland. Trevor Taylor led the smallest class with his Lotus Elite until brake trouble dropped him behind John Whitmore (Lotus Elite), Chris Lawrence (Morgan) and Clive Hunt (Lotus Elite).

Gilby Climax Type B

Post-war British motor racing was largely sustained by wealthy enthusiasts who supplied and maintained first-class racing machinery for our best drivers. Names spring to mind like John Coombs, Tommy Atkins, Tommy Sopwith, Rob Walker and, not least, Sid Greene. As a teenager he had lost his left arm in a road accident but was not prevented from becoming both racing driver and RAF fighter pilot. In 1953 he gave up competition driving and entered a Maserati A6GCS for Roy Salvadori, followed the year after by a Maserati 250F. When Salvadori departed, Greene concentrated on the racing career of his son Keith using Cooper and Lotus small-capacity sports cars. He then commissioned Len Terry to design a Climax-engined sports car which he named the Gilby after his engineering company. Encouraged by this first venture, a Formula 1 car was put in hand. Space-framed and Climax-engined, the car was run in UK F1 events plus the odd European race. Results were not startling but neither was the small team disgraced. A six-speed gearbox helped them to their best result with the Climax car – third in the 1962 Naples GP. A second chassis fitted with the BRM V8 engine was no improvement and the venture ceased when Gilby Engineering was sold.

The BRM-engined car was sold to Ian Raby who campaigned it in 1963 until the ex-works Brabham BT3 came along.

Len Terry's smart Gilby Climax F1 car at Goodwood on 23 April 1962.

Surtees was getting quicker, breaking the lap record, when he came up behind Jim Clark's Aston Martin at Madgwick. As Clark moved aside to let the leader through, the Aston got sideways and spun. Surtees was unable to avoid clouting the Aston amidships sending both cars off the road badly bent. Such an uncharacteristic mistake on Jim Clark's part was a puzzle. He may have been caught out by a puncture or his new rear tyres. Whatever the cause, Surtees's fine drive was at an end and a surprised Innes Ireland inherited the lead, chased by Mike Parkes (Ferrari), Graham Hill (Ferrari), Roy Salvadori (Jaguar) and David Piper (Ferrari). Robin Benson, driving Chris Kerrison's Ferrari 250GT SWB, added to Surtees's misery when he went off the road at the same place and further damaged both parked cars. Kerrison's Ferrari was the 250GT used by Stirling Moss to win the previous year's TT. It was subsequently rebodied by Drogo in 'bread van' form before being restored to its present glory in original configuration.

Parkes had a moment at Woodcote in his pursuit of Ireland and Graham Hill took second place as a result. Ireland slowed and Hill was closing at three seconds a lap, but the pale green Ferrari had enough in hand to win the race in a little over two and a half hours. Had it not been for the Easter crash, Stirling Moss would probably have driven that car, but we shall never know whether he would have won his eighth TT. At least we were sure that he was well on the way to recovery.

There had been no fewer than eight Members' Meetings during a hectic season which celebrated the BARC's golden jubilee. Their secretary, John Morgan, retired after 37 years with the club. Charles Meisl had arranged a championship for saloon cars, sponsored by the French lighting firm, Cibie. 'Doc' Merfield's Ford Anglia took first place by the narrowest of margins from joint runners-up Mike Cox and Mick Cave. The Brooklands Trophy went to Tony Hegbourne in his Lola Climax Mk 1.

Bill de Selincourt's
Lister Jaguar BHL103
leads away a mixed
field including Tony
Hegbourne's Lola Mk
1 BY-3 (28). *(24/3/62)*

Edward Portman's
Aston Martin DB4GT
Zagato 0177/R.
(24/3/62)

Roy Salvadori in the
Bowmaker/Yeoman
Lola Climax 4
BRGP43, fourth in the
Glover Trophy F1 race.
(24/3/62)

Bob Burnard wins the Veedol Championship in his AC Bristol BE1023 and with it a Lotus 22 Formula Junior car. *(18/8/62)*

Start of the 27th Tourist Trophy. Jim Clark is well under way from seventh in the Le Mans start while up front Innes Ireland has the Ferrari GTO (15) pointed up the road to victory. *(18/8/62)*

Sir Stirling Moss (1929–)

To summarise the brilliant career of Stirling Moss in a few lines would be impossible and his story has been widely written elsewhere. He is a man for whom the title 'Sporting Legend' is, for once, entirely appropriate. There are few names that are truly synonymous with their sport – Stanley Matthews, Don Bradman, Gordon Richards, Tiger Woods – but ask anyone to name a racing driver and the odds are that Stirling Moss will spring to the lips. He was one of the first British drivers to take a really serious approach to his racing. It was not that he failed to enjoy himself, but that his desire to do well led him to leave as little as possible to chance. He was thorough in his preparation and intelligently thoughtful in his planning. It was his ability (and willingness) to compete in a wide variety of cars and to succeed in them all that impressed. When, in 1955, he and Denis Jenkinson covered 1,000 miles of Italian roads in a fraction over 10 hours, few were surprised. Again, his supreme driving ability was enhanced by meticulous preparation and the inspired use of Jenks as navigator. From 500cc F3 to rallying, from the 'Monzanapolis' to Le Mans, he demonstrated his mastery in every type of car imaginable and earned the respect of the motor-racing world. He earned the tag 'the greatest driver never to win the world championship' but his was (and is!) a skill beyond the racking up of mere points. He was a driver who won innumerable races in superb style and always gave his very best.

An early picture of Stirling Moss.

1963

1963's Easter F1 race could muster a grid of only 10 cars. Significant was Reg Parnell's entry of a Lola Climax Mk 4 for 19-year-old New Zealander Chris Amon in his first European race. The finance companies had disappeared from the scene but the pale green remained under the British Racing Partnership banner with two Lotus 24s for Innes Ireland and future Chaparral creator, Jim Hall. Bruce McLaren had the new Cooper T66 using the latest short-stroke Coventry Climax V8 engine. Jack Brabham created his first Grand Prix car, the BT3, halfway through the 1962 season. The BT7 was on the way for 1963, Brabham recruiting Dan Gurney into his team, but the old BT3 was brought out again for Goodwood. There being no second Cooper for Tony Maggs he joined Amon in the Parnell team with a Lotus 24. BRMs were back with P57s for Graham Hill and Richie Ginther.

Graham Hill was on pole but Bruce McLaren led the first lap in the new and unpainted Cooper. Both Ginther and Hill passed him. Ginther waved the world champion past, then lost second place to McLaren. Brabham demoted Ginther one more place but then called at the pits with a loose ignition lead. Ginther departed with a rough-sounding engine and Hill lost his lead when the same fate befell him just five laps from the finish. Ireland had worked up to second and McLaren was too far adrift to challenge him. It was something of an inherited win but Innes Ireland was always a popular victor.

The works had all off-loaded their Formula Junior teams. Brabhams were entered by Ian Walker, Coopers by Ken Tyrrell, Lotus by Ron Harris and Lola by Midland Racing Partnership. There was a works Brabham Repco driven by Denny Hulme who was second on the grid and second in the race, but it was the Walker Brabham of Frank Gardner that won with Dickie Attwood's Lola third.

The St Mary's Trophy was the expected Jaguar benefit for Graham Hill, Roy Salvadori and Mike Salmon. The 2-litre class fell to the new Ford Cortina of

Jack Sears while Sir John Whitmore's works Mini Cooper beat Christabel Carlisle's in the 1000cc class.

John Coombs's E-type Jaguar 4WPD had been rebuilt as the first 'lightweight' car and at last enabled Graham Hill to beat Mike Parkes in the Maranello Ferrari 250GTO in the GT Race. Alan Hutcheson's MGB saw off the AC Bristols and Morgans, Sir John Whitmore had the quickest Lotus Elite and Andrew Hedges in Dick Jacobs's MG Midget took the 1200cc class.

Tommy Atkins had one of the latest Cooper Monaco T61Ms built for Roy Salvadori to drive. Powered by the Climax FPF 2700cc engine, the combination was virtually unbeatable during 1963 and the Easter sports car race success was one of many. The face of sports car racing was changing. The next three finishers came from the 1600cc class – Lotus Ford 23Bs driven by Alan Rees, Keith Greene and Mike Beckwith.

Another indication of the change in sports car racing, the feature 21-lap race at the Whitsun meeting, was for GT cars with sports cars in a supporting 15-lap event. The class of the GT field was obviously the Maranello Concessionaires team with two cars. Their original machine was driven by former works Cooper driver Mike MacDowel and a brand-new car was being run in during practice by Mike Parkes. Inevitably these two led from the start, initially MacDowel in front then Parkes took over to win with Chris Kerrison's rebodied 250GT third. Fourth was the first of the Lotus Elans driven by Graham Warner, the Elan starting to edge out the Elite in the 1600cc class. An impressive fifth was Warwick Banks in the Climax-engined Turner.

The coupé version of the Aston Martin DB3S made a rare appearance, driven by Peter Sutcliffe in the sports car race. The entry looked unbalanced as the larger-engined class was for cars over 1200cc and included, as well as the Aston, three D-type Jaguars and Chris Kerrison's 1220cc-engined Lola Mk 1. The fastest car in the class, in practice and in the race, was the Lotus 19 of John Coundley, driven by Bill de Selincourt.

The remainder of the field (those under 1200cc) was divided into two classes, up to and over 1000cc. The larger class was made up of Lotus 23, Lola Mk 1 and Elva Mk 7, with a single each of Terrier and DRW. The Climax engine was no longer the automatic choice with Ford power being chosen by many. The smaller class was all Ford-powered, chassis coming from Lotus (Mk 7), Merlyn (Mk 4), Terrier and Ginetta.

John Coundley drove the ex-Duncan Hamilton long-nosed D-type Jaguar into sixth place, the first finisher in the over-1200cc class behind winner de Selincourt. The Aston Martin was ninth and the Peter Skidmore D-type Jaguar fifteenth. These stalwarts of sports car racing were now past their sell-by dates and were being humbled by the the more modern, though more modestly powered, cars. Syd Fox finished second in the Neil Davis Lola Climax Mk 1 with Chris Williams's Lotus Ford 23 third, Robin Benson's Elva Climax Mk 7 fourth and Alistair Welch's Lotus Ford 23 fifth.

One thing that did not change was the historic race, won again by an ERA, this time Peter Waller in R9B. There was, however, a hint of a change even here. The race title referred to historic rather than pre-war racing cars and an A-type Connaught driven by Bob Salvage finished sixth, a car which raced at Goodwood in its heyday only 10 years earlier.

The 1963 Tourist Trophy meeting consisted of only two races. The Formula Junior championship fell to Peter Arundell's Ron Harris/Team Lotus Lotus Ford 27. He led from start to finish while his chief opponents, Richard Attwood in his Lola and Denny Hulme's Brabham, were busy fighting over second place.

Roy James had been consistently quick all season in his privately entered Brabham Ford BT6. He took part in the first practice session but then disappeared, much to the disappointment of Her Majesty's Constabulary who were anxious to discuss the Great Train Robbery and any part that James and his driving skills might have played in the escapade. Although James failed to reappear at Goodwood, it was noticeable that the constabulary maintained a strong presence throughout the meeting, all in the line of duty no doubt.

The Tourist Trophy was extended to 130 laps, about 3¼ hours of racing. Despite their withdrawal from racing, Aston Martin had continued development of the DB4GT with the so-called 'Project' cars. There were two DP214 cars on hand for Bruce McLaren and Innes Ireland but all was not well. The cars' Dunlop R6 tyres were fitted to rims an inch wider than the originals. These had been accepted at Le Mans and at Brands Hatch. It came as an unpleasant surprise to the team that the Goodwood scrutineer insisted that the cars revert to their original wheel size, thus narrowing the track and ruining the roadholding. The annoyance was increased because the same scrutineer had accepted them at Brands Hatch but refused them at Goodwood.

There was even more trouble with wheels and scrutineers. The AC Cobras entered by John Willment were rejected because of insufficient clearance between the wheels and steering arms. Replacement parts were summoned from America but failed to arrive in time and the cars were excluded. Jack Sears had already elected to drive John Coombs's Jaguar E-type but Bob Olthoff was left without a car to race.

The field was split into three classes with the Aston Martins and Jaguars in Class 1. It was widely expected that the winner would come from Class 2 which contained the Ferrari GTOs, the two Maranello cars for Graham Hill and Mike Parkes, David Piper in his own car, Roger Penske driving for the North American Racing Team and Prince Tchkotoua in the car crashed by John Surtees at the previous year's TT. It was ironic that His Highness was to repeat the accident at the same corner, severely damaging the car though without too much harm to his person. The class was completed by Chris Kerrison's rebodied 250GT, which had also played a part in that accident one year before.

Class 3 was by far the largest. Sir John Whitmore was to drive a Lotus Elan entered by SMART, the Stirling Moss Automobile Racing Team. It was good to see Stirling around the circuits again and no surprise that he was unable to remain idle and away from the sport that he loved. The Elans and Elites were matched against works supported Morgans and Dick Jacobs's immaculate MG Midgets. Goodwood veteran Dickie Stoop had forsaken Frazer Nash for the cars that they now imported and was always good value in his Porsche 356 Carrera.

The traditional Le Mans start had now been abandoned and the field lined up in 3x2x3 grid formation. In pole position was Graham Hill, Mike Parkes next to him, both in Maranello Ferrari 250GTOs. Third and fourth were Ireland and McLaren in the Aston Martins, despite their roadholding problems. Roy Salvadori was next in Tommy Atkins' lightweight E-type Jaguar. On the next row were Penske's Ferrari, Jack Sears in John Coombs's E-type and David Piper's GTO. John Whitmore was quickest of Class 3 in twelfth place on the grid.

Hill led off the grid in the red GTO with which Parkes had won at Whitsun. Parkes followed in the off-white car but was soon passed by Ireland, who was probably suffering something of the red-mist syndrome. He had equalled Hill's pole-setting time with the Aston Martin on 'proper' wheels and was not pleased to be pushed back to row two. Nor was he delighted with the way that the car now handled. This was emphasised when he tried to pass Hill at Woodcote, only to spin wildly. Those incorrect tyres now sported flat spots and Ireland called at the pits to change all four. A rumour spread that the team had swapped him back to those illegal wheels and a whole army of officials swooped on the car at the next pit stop only to be disappointed.

Ireland was a lap behind and found himself side by side with Parkes at the chicane. At considerably reduced speed they managed to squeeze through, only for Ireland to spin at Woodcote, delaying Parkes and allowing Hill to nip back into the lead. Parkes retook the place soon after though he slowed towards the end of the race and Hill went on to win. The Maranello drivers had agreed in advance that they would share the prize money and finishing first and second produced a mighty £700. Roy Salvadori brought the Atkins E-type home third with Jack Sears in the Coombs' E-type fourth. Next was David Piper's GTO with Dick Protheroe's E-type sixth. After a very fraught afternoon, Innes Ireland finished seventh.

Sir John Whitmore lost his class lead when a wheel fell off. Graham Warner took over but retired with a seized differential leaving class victory to Mike

Beckwith in jazzman Chris Barber's Elan. Dickie Stoop brought his Porsche home second in class with the Bob Duggan/Mike Johnson Lotus Elite third.

The final Members' Meeting of the year brought Ecurie Ecosse from Scotland to exercise their Cooper Monaco. Its young driver was scorchingly fast, lapping at a whisker under 100mph. Even driving the none too successful Tojeiro Coupe with 3½-litre Buick power he won his race against some serious opposition. It looked likely that Jimmy Stewart's younger brother Jackie might have a future in the sport.

Tim Mayer put his
Tyrrell Cooper T67 in
tenth place on the grid
for the Formula Junior
Championship but his
race ended in the
chicane wall. He was
stunned but not
seriously hurt.
(24/8/63)

Bruce McLaren retired
his ill-handling Aston
Martin DP214 on the
94th of 130 laps in the
Tourist Trophy.
(24/8/63)

Graham Hill's
victorious Ferrari
GTO leads Mike
Parkes' similar
second-placed car.
*(24/8/63 Photo: LAT
Photographic)*

Mini Cooper S

The Mini was introduced in 1959 as an economy car. Its competition potential was immediately apparent and John Cooper persuaded BMC to build 1,000 997cc-engined Cooper versions in order to homologate the car for saloon racing. BMC thought that they might struggle to sell 1,000 but they were wrong and the car was a huge success. 1963 saw the introduction of the Cooper 'S' with the engine enlarged to 1071cc, perhaps one of the most influential motor cars of all time. Racing and rallying were the cars' natural habitats. John Whitmore won the 1961 British Saloon Car Championship and he joined the BMC-backed Cooper Car Co. works team alongside John Love in 1962. The Monte Carlo Rally was a major sporting event capturing headlines throughout the world. Paddy Hopkirk's 1964 victory in the Mini Cooper established the car's reputation. Hopkirk joined the racing team for 1964. His team-mate was John Fitzpatrick, third of an illustrious line of Johns who drove for the works : Whitmore, Love, Fitzpatrick, Rhodes and Handley. Fitzpatrick finished second to Jim Clark in the UK championship while Warwick Banks cleaned up in the European Touring Car Championship. Timo Makinen won the 1965 Monte and BMC won six other major rallies with the Mini during that year.

Warwick Banks was joined in the works racing team by the latest John (Rhodes), the former winning the 1000cc class and the latter the 1300cc in the British championship. Not that the Cooper Car Co. cars had it all their own way: Minis prepared by the likes of Downton and Broadspeed often featured in the results. Paddy Hopkirk won the 1966 Monte but was then disqualified (together with the second and third finishing Minis) over alleged headlight irregularities. Although an outrage at the time, it certainly gained BMC more publicity than an unchallenged win. The Monte fell to Mini again in 1967 (Rauno Aaltonen) but the cars international racing heyday came to an end in 1968 with John Handley winning the European championship 1000cc class and John Rhodes the 1600cc class. Minis are still raced all over the world despite the fact that Alec Issigonis had no intention of producing a competition car – perhaps the ultimate tribute to what was conceived as an economy runabout.

Mini battle between John Love's works 997cc Morris and John Whitmore's similar Austin model. Both cars threw tyre treads and Christabel Carlisle won the class.

Graham Hill (1929–1975)

After his engineering apprenticeship, Graham Hill served in the Royal Navy. An accomplished oarsman, racing on dry land also appealed and he found a job with a racing drivers' school. He first raced in a F3 Cooper at Brands Hatch in 1954, later that year hitching a lift with Colin Chapman and talking his way into a mechanics job with the Lotus team, working for Dick Steed and Dan Margulies in exchange for the occasional drive. Chapman realised that he was rather more than a mechanic who could drive a bit and 1956 saw a few works drives and guest appearances in other owner's cars. He joined Speedwell Conversions, driving their tuned Austin A35s, but was back at Lotus in 1958 for his first GP in a Lotus 12. This was followed by the 16 but neither brought great success and he departed to BRM. The next two years saw a lot of hard work and some encouraging top six finishes but it was 1962 when the team were told 'succeed or quit' that he took the V8-engined P57 to four GP wins and the world championship. Four more years at BRM saw him win three successive Monaco and US GPs. Sports, GT and saloon victories also came with John Coombs, Porsche, Maranello and others. Then in 1966 (the year of his Indianapolis victory) it was back to Lotus to join Jim Clark and in 1967 came the Cosworth DFV engine. They were the team to beat but with Clark's untimely death in 1968, Hill became team leader, and with three GP wins came his second championship. It was Stewart's year in 1969 and it ended with Hill crashing at Watkins Glen and smashing both legs. Though almost

unable to walk, he was behind the wheel of Rob Walker's Lotus at the start of 1970 though the season yielded little. He drove for Brabham in 1971 and 1972 with unremarkable results but he did win Le Mans for Matra in 1972. He formed his own team in 1973, racing Lolas and Shadows through 1974. He built his own car in 1975 but decided to retire after failing to qualify at Monaco. He concentrated on the team, in particular the hugely promising Tony Brise, but tragedy intervened when an aircraft, piloted by Hill, crashed in fog killing Hill, Brise and four other team members. This witty man was admired by the enthusiasts for the way that he grafted to achieve his ambition and the public widely mourned a people's champion.

Graham Hill sports his rowing club colours on his helmet.

1964

1964 saw the demise of Formula Junior and the introduction of a new Formula 3 for 1000cc single-seaters. Ken Tyrrell was again entering what were effectively the works Coopers and he had secured the services of Jackie Stewart and Warwick Banks. The Cooper with BMC power was not the quickest F3 car, but Stewart was unbeatable all season and started by leading the Easter meeting Chichester Cup race from pole to flag. Warwick Banks, himself a very fast driver, spent the race swapping second place with John Fenning's Lotus BMC 22. The Lotus driver finally took the runner up position some 14 seconds behind Stewart.

The Jaguars had finally been eclipsed by US muscle. The saloon car race saw only two of the Coventry cars entered against three 7-litre Ford Galaxies. Though both Jack Brabham and Sir Gawaine Baillie non-started, the remaining car swept Jack Sears to victory. Only six seconds behind was the wheel-waving Ford Lotus Cortina of Jim Clark, followed by the similar cars of teammate Peter Arundell, Frank Gardner and Bob Olthoff driving John Willment's cars.

The Jaguars, only fractionally faster than the Mini Coopers, were both excluded from the results. All the drivers objected to being asked to sign declarations that their cars conformed with the regulations. The stewards withdrew this requirement on condition that any car failing post-race scrutineering would be excluded. The Jaguars did not turn up for inspection.

Another upset was caused by Mike Young in the Superspeed Ford Anglia, which beat all the Minis. Indeed, the works Mini Coopers finished behind the Minis tuned by Alexander Engineering and Downton Engineering.

The entry for the Formula 1 race looked more healthy than the previous year. The race had a new sponsor in *The News of the World* newspaper and, but for the absence of Ferrari, would not have disgraced a Grand Prix. Team Lotus fielded two of the seminal monocoque-chassised 25s for Jim Clark and Peter Arundell. The Lotus was powered by the Coventry Climax V8, as were the rest of the field apart from those using the BRM V8, which was as popular among the private teams.

BRM themselves had a new car, the P261, but only one chassis was available to Graham Hill, Richard Attwood being left with the P57, which had proved such a friend to Hill that it became known as 'Old Faithful'. There should have been two of the new P261s but the other chassis had been severely bent in Hill's accident at the earlier Snetterton meeting. Jack Brabham also had a new car, the BT7. A second car was provisionally entered but later withdrawn. In a similar situation were Coopers, who had one of the previous year's T66s available for Bruce McLaren but the second provisional entry was withdrawn. McLaren's 1964 teammate was to be Phil Hill but he would not drive for the team until the Aintree 200 three weeks later. A familiar name returned with the Bob Gerard-entered Cooper T59 for John Taylor. This was a 1962 Formula Junior chassis with a Lotus (Cosworth) Ford engine in the back.

British Racing Partnership had ex-Lotus drivers Trevor Taylor in a Lotus 24 with BRM power and Innes Ireland with their own BRP BRM. Rob Walker was back with Cooper for Jo Bonnier. Reg Parnell Racing had their own Lotus 25 BRM for motorcycling great Mike Hailwood, and from America came Peter Revson with one of the Parnell-built Lotus 24s, BRM powered and wearing a Lola Mk 4 body. Ian Raby had swapped the Gilby F1 car for Jack Brabham's original BT3. Belgian André Pilette had a Scirocco Climax which began life as one of the Emeryson F1 cars. The field was completed by the return of Scuderia Centro Sud. There were no Maseratis for them but their BRM P57 was painted red and driven by Giancarlo Baghetti, who had made motor-racing history by winning the first Grand Prix in which he took part, the 1961 French GP.

Jack Brabham had lapped a second under the lap record in practice. Jim Clark was second on the grid with the front row completed by Graham Hill's BRM. Peter Arundell and Innes Ireland occupied the second row. Clark made the quickest start but Hill led out of Madgwick with Clark, Brabham and Ireland on his tail. Ireland dropped back from the leading group and was joined by Arundell and McLaren. Richard Attwood, Trevor Taylor and Jo Bonnier formed the next trio, John Taylor circulated on his own ahead of yet another trio of Baghetti, Hailwood and Raby. Bernard Collomb (Lotus Climax 24) and André Pilette brought up the rear. There were five groups all engaged in their own races. From fastest to slowest, there were contests to watch right through the field. For his 10 shilling admission charge, the 1960s spectator got a lot of racing.

The leading trio held station but Arundell had designs on fourth place and tried overtaking Ireland on the inside of Madgwick. Innes braked hard, spun and took McLaren with him into the bank. Clark made his charge on Hill but the Lotus clutch gave out and he dropped back into the clutches of a grateful Brabham who took second place. This was short lived as the wheel rim supporting the new 13-inch Dunlop racing tyres split. This left the Brabham as yet another car involuntarily parked against the Madgwick bank. Hill's safe lead then disappeared as he coasted into the pits with a broken distributor arm. Jim Clark inherited a fortunate win, followed home by teammate Peter Arundell with Trevor Taylor making it a Lotus 1-2-3. Richard Attwood brought the older BRM home fourth after a steady drive.

Graham Hill's consolation prize came with victory in the GT race driving the Maranello Ferrari GTO, re-bodied in GTO/64 style. To win he had to fight his way past Jack Sears in the Willment 4.7-litre AC Cobra and he had to drive mighty fast to stay ahead.

The final race, for sports cars, lost most of its interest when both Jim Clark in the 4.7-litre Lotus Ford 30 and the Ecurie Ecosse Tojeiro Buick non-started. John Coundley's Lotus Climax 19 beat Jackie Stewart's Ecosse Cooper Monaco with Jack Brabham's BRM-engined Brabham BT8 third. His duel with Tony Lanfranchi's Elva BMW 7 was the highlight of the race. It was therefore doubly disappointing when Brabham was excluded because his windscreen wiper did not work. There was also a problem with his fuel tank, which was within the car's cockpit. Fortunately, Brabham was reinstated on appeal but then Lanfranchi was excluded on similar grounds. His appeal did not succeed. There were other disqualifications, making it plain that motor racing was becoming a very serious business.

For several years, the Crystal Palace Whitsun meeting had taken precedence over the Goodwood event on the same day. British motor racing had changed greatly over the last decade, works teams and Grand Prix drivers appearing less at those meetings that did not have 'international' status. Roy Salvadori had always taken every opportunity to race wherever he could and rarely missed a Goodwood meeting. He took the 1964 Whitsun trophy in the Atkins Cooper Monaco T61P – the latest variation on the theme, now with 5-litre Maserati power. Bob Olthoff also put a 'big banger' at the front of the GT class with the Willment-entered AC Cobra.

Winner of the 1100cc GT class was Graham Capel. He had the neat idea of adding a roof to the good old Lotus Eleven. It was duly homologated as the last Elevens had chassis numbers into the 500s, though it later became clear that rather less than this number had been built. This hardly matters as it extended the life of this delightful car and tested the ingenuity of those who followed suit with GT conversions.

Goodwood hero Reg Parnell had died tragically young. He had greatly influenced post-war motor racing in the UK. His long run of successes in the early Goodwood races made it particularly fitting that his widow, Betty, should present a trophy in his name to the BARC. The first award of the trophy was for the 1964 Whitsun Formula 3 race and the first recipient was Roger Mac, who had enjoyed a very successful season in the club meetings driving his Brabham BT6.

What was to be the final Goodwood Tourist Trophy race took place on 29 August 1964. Contenders in the World GT Championship were to be mixed with sports racing cars. It was decided to support the main event with a race for under 2-litre GT cars, thus keeping the slower runners out of the way of the much quicker TT entries. The support race, over 21 laps, fell to Mike Spence in the Lotus Elan entered by the Chequered Flag team. Second came Goodwood stalwart Dickie Stoop in his Porsche 904 followed by Mike de'Udy's similar car.

The Tourist Trophy entry suggested an exciting contest both in the sports and GT categories. Fastest in practice was Bruce McLaren in the rebodied F1 Cooper with Oldsmobile engine that he had bought from Roger Penske. Hot on his heels was Jim Clark in the works Lotus 30 with a 4727cc Ford engine. Completing the front row of the grid was Graham Hill in the Maranello Ferrari 330P. The second row was shared by airline pilot Hugh Dibley in the Stirling Moss-entered Brabham BT8 with 2½-litre Climax power and the similar Team Elite 2-litre car of Denny Hulme.

The GT class was equally enthralling. The American-engineered AC Cobras had a good chance of displacing Ferrari as GT champions. Carroll Shelby brought over two of the magnificent Daytona Coupés for Dan Gurney and Phil Hill. These were supported by three open cars for Jack Sears and Bob Olthoff (Willment) and Roy Salvadori (Atkins). The North American Racing Team brought over a Ferrari 250GTO for John Surtees. There were similar cars for Richie Ginther and Innes Ireland (Maranello) and Tony Maggs (Piper). Peter Lumsden had tried the Lindner lightweight E-type Jaguar during practice and crashed it, leaving Peter Nocker without a drive. Lumsden was still able to drive his own car, as were Peter Sutcliffe and Roger Mac. Only one Aston Martin attended – the Project 214 car of Mike Salmon.

McLaren took off in the lead from Clark and Hulme. On lap eight, Ireland clipped Roger Nathan's Brabham at St Mary's and spun. Tony Lanfranchi, following in his Elva BMW 7, stood on his brakes and was charged from behind by the Surtees GTO. The Ferrari rode up the Elva and was launched into the bank. Surtees suffered concussion and Ireland pitted to have bodywork levered off a wheel. Jack Sears had dropped to the back of the field after a spin.

Jim Clark took the lead when McLaren was forced out with clutch trouble. Denny Hulme (Brabham) and Trevor Taylor (Elva) followed with Graham Hill (Ferrari) fourth until a spin put him back a place. This certainly caught his attention as he not only took back his place but also passed Taylor and set his sights on Hulme.

The GT class was led by Salvadori (Cobra) until he, too, was caught out by a spin. Carroll Shelby in the Cobra pit was quite content to allow the British Cobra teams to do the winning on their home ground but, when Salvadori lost the GT class lead, he hung out the 'GO' sign to Dan Gurney, who obligingly put the hammer well and truly down. Phil Hill suffered an early setback when a stone punctured an oil cooler but the 1961 world champion was still motoring in determined fashion.

Graham Hill finally got past Denny Hulme and found himself leading when Jim Clark stopped unexpectedly early for fuel. He was back out only briefly before another pit stop for more fuel. The Lotus was failing to pick up out of the corners. Hill now had a lead of a whole minute but Clark pursued him with the Lotus now seeming on song again. He was closing sufficiently quickly to give him a chance for victory when a front wishbone gave out and his race came to an end. Meanwhile David Piper had taken third (now second) place in his Ferrari 250LM and Dan Gurney had the Daytona Cobra next and leading the GT class. Jack Sears and Bob Olthoff followed in the Willment Cobras to give Shelby a 1-2-3.

Despite the excellent race the crowd was small and the Tourist Trophy would move on to Oulton Park. The last of Goodwood's classic sports car races had been run.

Lotus Climax 25

Monocoque construction had been seen before but Colin Chapman introduced the concept to Grand Prix racing with his Lotus 25. Instead of the tangle of tubing which produced the traditional space frame, the driver sat in a 'bathtub' of two backbones linked by an undertray with bulkheads back and front. This structure resulted in a light, stiff chassis which permitted softer suspension resulting in better road-holding on slower corners, the stiffer chassis more accurately locating the independent suspension. Fuel was carried in rubber bags inside the side pontoons. The whole car was as low and narrow as the construction method would allow, resulting in what Chapman described as 'quite the cleanest and nicest-looking car we'd ever made'. Customers who had bought the space frame Lotus 24 were not amused to be out-performed by the innovative 25 which carried Jim Clark to his first world championship and also brought Lotus the manufacturers' prize in 1963, their first success, though Clark was narrowly beaten by Graham Hill in 1962. Recording 14 world championship GP and 11 non-championship wins during a long career, the cars also provided the backbone for the Parnell team, although they used BRM power. Steadily developed, the car evolved into the Lotus 33 which proved as dominant, winning Jim Clark his 1965 championship.

Jim Clark in the winning Lotus Climax 25 on Easter Monday 1964. *(Photo: LAT Photographic)*

David Beckett sails
bravely onwards in
Lister Jaguar BHL125
on his way to second
place in the previously
Chevrolet-powered car.
(14/3/64)

Almost swamped is
Godfrey Lambert's
Cooper Ford, eighth in
the Formule Libre race.
Goodwood was not
always glorious.
(14/3/64)

Richard Burton's Lotus
Ford 31 Formula 3 car
managed fourth place
in the Formule Libre
race. *(14/3/64)*

Jim Clark's driving of
the Lotus Cortina is
the stuff of legend.
Here he three-wheels
through the chicane
ahead of Peter
Sutcliffe's Austin
Cooper S. *(30/3/64)*

Jackie Stewart
impressed in Ken
Tyrrell's Formula 3
Cooper Austin.
*(30/3/64 Photo: LAT
Photographic)*

Bruce McLaren in his
ex-F1 Cooper/ex-Zerex
Special now officially
Cooper Oldsmobile
but, in reality, the start
of the McLaren line of
race cars. He was
fastest in practice but
retired from the
Tourist Trophy.
(29/8/64)

A Shelby pit stop and Dan Gurney seems unsure that this is all a good idea as he prepares to take on Daytona Cobra CSX2299 in the Tourist Trophy. *(29/8/64)*

Jim Clark in Lotus Climax 25 R6 leads Jack Brabham's BT7-2-63 into Woodcote corner. *(30/3/64)*

Hugh Dibley explains
to John Bolster why the
Stirling Moss
Automobile Racing
Team Brabham Climax
BT8 lasted only two
laps of the Tourist
Trophy. *(29/8/64)*

Jim Clark looks less
than thrilled with the
Lotus 30, which
dropped from the lead
with fuel and
suspension bothers.
Colin Chapman (dark
glasses) thinks his own
thoughts. *(29/8/64)*

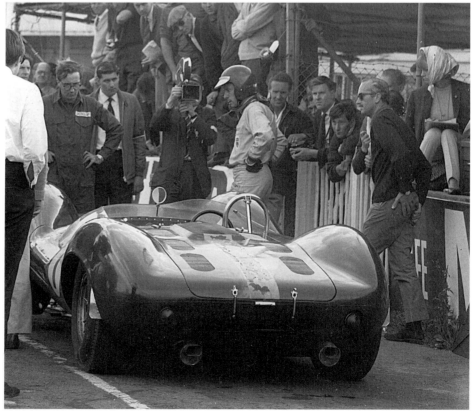

Bob Olthoff powers
John Willment's Lotus
Cortina through the
chicane pursued by
two more of the same
model. *(30/3/64)*

The home-grown
Cobras played their
part. Roy Salvadori
with HEM-6. *(29/8/64)*

215

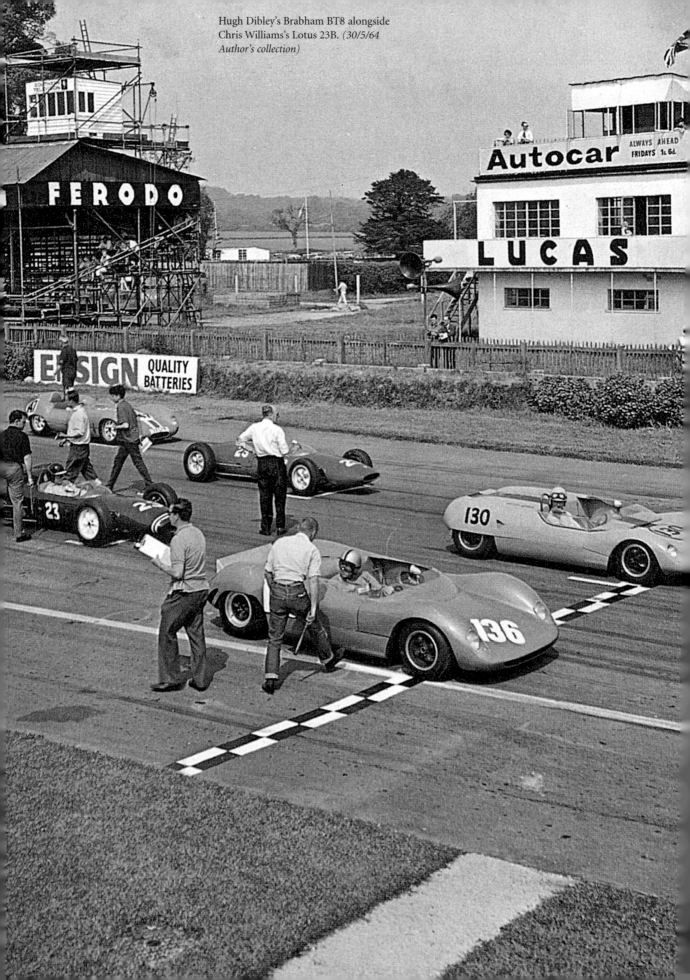

Hugh Dibley's Brabham BT8 alongside
Chris Williams's Lotus 23B. *(30/5/64
Author's collection)*

Jim Clark is interviewed by Raymond Baxter.

Jim Clark (1936–1968)

Son of a Scottish farmer, Jim Clark was a naturally talented driver who needed persuading of the greatness of his own skills. After local events he took part in his first race meeting in June 1956 but began to come to notice behind the wheel of friend Ian Scott-Watson's Porsche 1600S in 1957. Driving the Border Reivers' D-type Jaguar in 1958 he won a dozen races. He impressed Colin Chapman when he drove Scott-Watson's Lotus Elite and even more so when he scored another dozen wins in the Reivers' Lister Jaguar in 1959. Reg Parnell signed Clark for the Aston Martin F1 team in 1960 but the car was long delayed and Clark was released to drive FJ and F2 Team Lotus cars. Thus began his relationship with Chapman, which would result in world championships in 1963 and 1965. He won Indianapolis in 1965 but 1966 saw frustration with the BRM H16-engined Lotus. The advent of the Lotus 49 and Cosworth DFV in 1967 resulted in some of the Scot's greatest drives but, as in 1962 and 1964, he narrowly missed the title. 1968 started well but, in the opening round of the European F2 Championship at Hockenheim, he slid inexplicably off the road and was fatally injured when the car struck a tree. This quiet, modest man was greatly mourned by the racing world. He will be remembered not only for his skill at the wheel of a GP car but by those who saw him three-wheeling a Lotus Cortina or taming the Lotus 30.

1965

1965 was to be Goodwood's last full season and would see the circuit's final Formula 1 race. Easter was quite late that year, Easter Monday falling on 19 April. Memory blesses all Goodwood meetings with bright sun and blue skies but this is a trick of nostalgia. Certainly those who braved the elements that Bank Holiday will not forget the driving hail storm which greeted the start of the first race. After one lap the black flag was shown and the field sent back to the paddock. Though the gale blew the storm away, the race finally took place on a streaming wet track and visibility was negligible. Cars collided or simply spun on their own and through it all came winner Roy Pike in the Chequered Flag Brabham Ford BT16 with Piers Courage in his wake in the Charles Lucas Brabham Ford BT10.

By now the programme was well behind schedule and the St Mary's Trophy saloon race was reduced from 10 to five laps. It was no small achievement that Mike Salmon and Roy Pierpoint managed to finish third and fourth in Ford Mustangs, which must have felt like oil tankers in the pouring rain which had now replaced the hail. It was no surprise that Jim Clark and Jack Sears brought Team Lotus a 1-2 in their Lotus Cortinas. What had been a surprise was John Rhodes in third place with the works Cooper S, but his superb drive was rewarded by a penalty for a jumped start.

It was some consolation to the soaked and freezing spectators that the skies cleared for the Formula 1 race, sponsored this year by the *Sunday Mirror*. The BRMs were fastest in practice but it was the young Jackie Stewart who pushed team-mate Graham Hill into second position. Team Lotus came next in the order Jim Clark and Mike Spence. Fifth fastest was Bob Anderson in his privately entered Brabham Climax BT11, quicker than Jack Brabham's works car and Bruce McLaren's Cooper Climax T77. Dan Gurney's second works Brabham was followed by Jo Bonnier and Jo Siffert in the Rob Walker-entered Brabham Climax BT7s.

Mike Spence had the Lotus Climax 33 fuel-injection pack up on the warm-up lap, leaving space in the second row which Dan Gurney used to good effect, following Graham Hill and Jim Clark into Madgwick on the first lap. Clark took six laps to take a lead that he would not lose. Behind him Gurney and Stewart passed Hill but then both retired on the same lap, leaving the BRM team leader to take second place, 24 seconds behind Clark. Bob Anderson was disqualified for missing the chicane, somewhat unfairly since he actually went clean through the wooden section when his brakes failed. Even less fortunate was Jo Siffert who hit the brick section at the same corner. The car disintegrated and he was lucky to escape with cuts and bruises.

Roger Mac won the GT race in the Chequered Flag AC Cobra from Jack Sears's Willment-entered Cobra Coupé. Jim Clark (Lotus Ford 30) scored his hat-trick in the sports car race ahead of Bruce McLaren's first creation, the McLaren Oldsmobile M1A, David Hobbs (Lola Chevrolet T70) and Hugh Dibley (Lola Chevrolet T70). Engine sizes ranged from 4500cc to 5960cc. Clark left the sports car lap record at 106.93mph.

In marked contrast to Easter, the Whitsun meeting really did take place under blue skies, a suitable farewell setting for one of Goodwood's most successful drivers, Roy Salvadori. In addition to Maranello Concessionaires, Col. Ronnie Hoare also had an interest in Ford dealers F. English Ltd. They provided a new Ford GT40 for Salvadori who had done much of the development testing for Ford. It would have been fitting had he won but that was asking a little much against the McLaren Oldsmobile M1A of John Coundley and the Brabham Oldsmobile BT8 of Roger Nathan. The Brabham dropped out and Salvadori finished second in the last race of a magnificent career.

Roger Mac won the GT class, a repetition of his Easter success, in the Chequered Flag Cobra. Second was Peter Lumsden's E-type Jaguar but Mike Salmon retired his Ferrari 250GTO/64 early in the race. He made up for this with a win in the saloon race with his Ford Mustang. Mick Cave was indecently fast in his Austin A40, defeating all the Mini Cooper S opponents in the 1300cc class. Nick Brittan completed the Mini humiliation by winning the 1000cc class in his Ford Anglia.

The Formula 3 Reg Parnell Trophy Race fell to Piers Courage in his Charles Lucas Brabham BT10. The historic race was marked by the return of the Maserati 250F. Colin Crabbe's 250F was leading till the last lap when he slowed dramatically and was overtaken by Bob Salvage (Connaught A-type) and only just headed Patrick Lindsay's ERA R5B across the line.

The last Members' Meeting of the season was staged on 3 July and there were no further meetings that year, perhaps hinting at the circuit's doubtful future. 1966 would see the introduction of a new Formula 1 for 3-litre cars,

twice the capacity of the existing F1. The future of sports-car racing had already been seen with the introduction of 'big banger' American engines. Goodwood had an enviable safety record. Drivers had been killed, but at a time when this was an accepted penalty of the sport. The public had been unharmed and this was no mean achievement.

David Cole's Brabham Ford BT15, winner of the Formula 3 race. *(3/7/65)*

Jim Clark acknowledges the chequered flag at the close of Goodwood's last Formula 1 race. *(19/4/65)*

Start of the *Sunday Mirror* Formula 1 race. Jackie Stewart's BRM P261 is beside Graham Hill's sister car with Bob Anderson (Brabham BT11), Dan Gurney (Brabham BT11), Bruce McLaren (Cooper T77), Jo Bonnier (Brabham BT7) and the rest of the field formed up behind. *(19/4/65)*

Lotus Ford 30

Colin Chapman's Lotus 30 was one of the first British-built American-engined sports cars, but perhaps the least successful, although some present-day opinion has it that the car was merely under-developed. Built on a central backbone chassis similar to the Elan, the car was powered by Ford (unsurprisingly) in the form of their V8 4727cc unit.

1965 saw the introduction of the much-revised Series 2 model. The chassis was considerably stiffer and an upswept tail spoiler improved road-holding. The Easter 1965 Lavant Cup win was one of the highlights of the year, as new cars from McLaren and Lola put the Lotus in the shade. Lotus produced the new 40 in an effort to keep up. Even a 5754cc engine hardly improved its performance and Chapman quietly shelved the venture.

Jim Clark won the Lavant Cup Race in the works Lotus Ford 30/S2/1.

Sir Jackie Stewart (1939–)

Denis Jenkinson had a theory that the greatest drivers all have unusual eyes. He proposed that perhaps the eyes were unusual in appearance because they were also unusual in operation, that they were particularly keen and that this might be linked to especially fast reactions. Jackie Stewart certainly has very bright and piercing eyes and those that watched him early in his career had no doubt that he had lightning reactions. His early interest was shooting, at which he also excelled, but he must have been influenced by his elder brother Jimmy, a driver of similar talent whose career was cut short by an accident in 1955. Jackie's early success at club level was rewarded with regular drives for Ecurie Ecosse and Ken Tyrrell's F3 Cooper team. He turned down Lotus in favour of BRM for his F1 season in 1965. He stayed with the team for three seasons, winning two GPs, but moving to the Ken Tyrrell-run Matras in 1968 and his first world championship in 1969. In 1971 came the first Tyrrell-built car and another world championship. A lay-off with an ulcer inter-rupted 1972 but 1973 saw him at his very best. He planned retirement at the season's end when he reached his hundredth GP but he withdrew from that last race when teammate François Cevert died in a practice crash. Stewart's 27 GP wins exceeded those of his hero Jim Clark. His tireless crusade for driver safety did not endear him to those who regarded the

danger as an inherent part of the sport, but the relative safety of motor racing today is due in no small measure to his efforts. He continued to use his considerable intelligence at work in the motoring world.

He supported his son Paul's team and finally brought it into GP racing in 1997, their success tempting Ford to buy out the operation as the basis for their new Jaguar team.

Jackie Stewart in his early days as BRM works driver.

1966

GOODWOOD faced an insurmountable problem. The circuit was surrounded by public roads and there was no space available to move spectators further from the action. It could also be that the Duke of Richmond was out of tune with the direction that motor racing was taking and would not be sorry to see it move out of his 'back garden'. However, the 1966 season started without any announcement about Goodwood's future. There would be no Formula 1 cars or 'big banger' sports cars and perhaps that alone should have told us that the circuit's days were numbered.

Ironically, a Formula 1 race at Easter 1966 would have produced a very thin field, whereas its Formula 2 substitute brought a first-class line-up. Of great interest – and significance for motor racing far into the future – were the Brabham BT18s with Honda power for Jack Brabham and Denny Hulme. They were second and first, respectively, in practice. The Team Lotus Ron Harris-run Lotus Cosworth 35s were handled by Jim Clark and Peter Arundell. Ken Tyrrell had begun his association with Matra, Jackie Stewart and Jackie Ickx having a choice of BRM or Cosworth powered MS5s. Matra themselves entered BRM-engined works cars for Jean-Pierre Beltoise and Jo Schlesser.

Graham Hill, Trevor Taylor, Jochen Rindt, Alan Rees, David Prophet, Bill Bradley, Roger Mac and Ian Raby were among the drivers of a host of privately entered Brabhams. Richard Attwood and Frank Gardner drove the Midland Racing Partnership Lola Cosworth 61s while Jo Siffert and Bob Anderson had Cooper T82s.

As the grid formed up, Jim Clark's engine was misfiring. The team had only just finished fitting a new drive shaft to Arundell's car, but as he drew up on the grid he found himself transferred to Clark's car. As the flag fell, the Brabhams scorched off into the lead followed by Stewart, Hill, Clark and

Rindt – six world champions in a row. This may have been Formula 2, but it was certainly not second rate.

Rindt passed Clark, who promptly retook the place and got past Graham Hill for good measure. Hill's engine started to go off song, then Clark retired with a puncture followed by Arundell, the misfire in Clark's original car becoming terminal. Stewart was chasing Brabham and Hulme when he suffered an almighty spin at Lavant corner. His car had been grounding over the new concrete kerbs at the chicane and part of the throttle mechanism had worn away. The throttle stuck open with dramatic results. He managed to get back to the pits where the car was retired. Ken Tyrrell called in Jackie Ickx and Stewart took over the BRM-engined car. Restarting in tenth place he made it to sixth at the finish.

Brabham and Hulme completed their untroubled run and were followed home by Jochen Rindt and Alan Rees in the Winkelmann-entered BT18s and Graham Hill in the John Coombs BT16 to complete a Brabham rout.

The imposition of a 3-litre limit on GT cars disqualified the E-type Jaguar and the Cobra, leaving a very thin field from which John Miles's Willment-entered Lotus Elan proved the winner. Similarly, the Lavant Cup sports car race had no entries over 2 litres. The race further suffered from 16 non-starters and four retirements, leaving only 10 runners. Of these, several potential winners had mechanical problems and it was Mike Spence in the one-off Parnell BRM who won from Tony Dean's Brabham Climax BT8. Third came Mac Daghorn driving the innovative Felday BRM four-wheel drive machine. Another rare beast was fourth, Mike Beckwith in the Willment BRM.

This was Goodwood's final international event, played out before a small crowd. There was more choice available. On the same day there had been meetings at Brands Hatch, Silverstone and Castle Combe. Without the draw of Formula 1, spectators could pick the most convenient circuit rather than travel to the far south of the country. The May/June issue of the bi-monthly BARC Gazette stated that, although the club had applied to run the 1967 Easter meeting at Silverstone, there was no intention of closing Goodwood and national dates would be applied for at Easter and Whitsun 1967, together with a series of Members' Meetings. This may well have been the genuine intention but a mix of National and Members' Meetings would not have proved financially viable for very long.

There were just three Members' Meetings in the 1966 season. The very last public meeting was run at Whitsun on a gloriously sunny day. The main event was the Reg Parnell Formula 3 race, which was almost won by local hero Derek Bell. He had already distinguished himself by winning his very first race at Goodwood when he steered his Lotus Seven through such appalling conditions that he was more surprised than anyone to find himself the victor.

Jackie Stewart in the Formula 2 Matra at the final international meeting at the Sussex circuit. *(11/4/66 Photo: LAT Photographic)*

Now he was racing his own Lotus Ford 41 F3 car to great effect, but was pipped on this day by David Cole's Brabham Ford BT18.

Tony Dean scored a pole-to-flag win in the supporting sports car race driving his Brabham Climax BT8, followed by John Miles in the Willment Lotus Elan. Alan Peer took the saloon race in his Ford Anglia and the marque race fell to Chris Lawrence's Morgan.

It was fitting that the last race should be for historic cars. Maserati 250Fs, Connaught A-types and, of course, ERAs all stirred the memories of those who had enjoyed such great racing at Goodwood for 18 years, a period during which British cars and drivers had come to the fore and established a place on the international scene which they would not relinquish. It was also fitting that Peter Brewer should win the last race in an Aston Martin.

On 2 July the 71st and last Members' Meeting took place. The final race was won by Dickie Metcalfe in his Lola Climax Mk 1. He had raced at the very first meeting in 1948 and at many in between.

The July/August BARC Gazette carried the headline on its front page 'Goodbye, Goodwood'.

Brabham Honda BT18

1966 was a good year for Jack Brabham. It ended with his third world championship, won in a car carrying his own name as constructor. His cars were winning in Indy racing and Formula 3, and totally dominating Formula 2. Jack had spent a year nurturing his connection with the Honda factory and easing them into competition engine production. The car won at its first outing, the Goodwood Easter 1966 feature race. In fact Jack and Denny Hulme finished first and second, admitting that their Honda engines gave them an enormous advantage over their opponents. They proceeded to win every F2 race of the year. They were often followed home by other Brabhams but with Ford power, Honda engines being restricted to the works team. Other teams would have been delighted to get their hands on a Honda unit but the factory was faithful to Jack, even offering him their F1 engine for 1967, a deal that went to John Surtees when Jack confirmed his loyalty to Repco, who had given him his winning power in 1966. Honda's introduction to European motor racing has repercussions echoing through the sport to this day, their contribution being matched by their success.

Jack Brabham in the Honda-powered Formula 2 Brabham winning Goodwood's final Easter Monday feature race at the last international meeting. *(Photo: LAT Photographic)*

Sir Jack Brabham (1926–)

After success in his native Australia with a Cooper Bristol, Jack Brabham came to England in 1955 and soon found a home with the Cooper team. It was not driving skill alone that he brought to the team and Coopers benefited considerably from his engineering abilities. Two world championships later and Jack was running his own team and building his own cars. With Dan Gurney in the team, Jack concentrated on development but, with a new formula, 1966 was to see him as champion once again, this time in a car bearing his own name, the first driver to do so. He also swept the board in the F2 Brabham Honda, making 1966 his most successful year. It was second driver Denny Hulme's year in 1967 and the world champion was once again driving a Brabham car. The 1968 season was a disaster but 1969 saw DFV power and new team driver Jackie Ickx restore good order though not great success. His final year, 1970, saw a win in South Africa and two GPs (Britain and Monaco) lost on the last corner. Though his skills were undiminished he sold up and left the sport, though he is still a welcome visitor to historic meetings around the world.

Thoughtful as ever, Jack Brabham let his driving speak for him.

Postscript

WHEN THE gates closed for the last time we wondered what the circuit's future was to be. Would it be allowed to crumble slowly away, or, worse still, would it become an industrial estate or business park? It is truly remarkable that the circuit remained intact and cared for over the next 32 years. During that time the circuit was rarely out of use. Most weekends saw sprints or club gatherings. During the week major teams would be testing their cars. Noise limitations were imposed in 1974 which meant the fitting of silencers. Nevertheless, even Formula 1 teams continued to test there into the 1980s. Bruce McLaren lost his life testing his CanAm McLaren in 1970 and Bertrand Fabi died during a test session in 1989. After this, the larger teams tested elsewhere. The airfield within the circuit was in constant use. Driving tuition, both for road and track, corporate entertaining, club track days and numerous other activities were added to the still regular sprints and rally stages.

Grandson of the circuit's founder, the present Earl of March had always hoped to bring racing back to the Goodwood circuit. Following the great success of the Festival of Speed, an event based around a hillclimb up the drive of Goodwood House, Lord March put forward his plans for historic racing at the circuit. Housing had spread closer to the circuit and there was the inevitable local concern about noise and congestion. This was countered by the Goodwood Supporter's Association, which promoted the undoubted advantages to the local economy that carefully planned events would bring. Eventually the local council accepted the Earl's proposals in return for a restriction on other activities at the circuit and careful monitoring of noise levels. Noise was to be damped by the erection of large earth banks, which also provided even better spectator viewing than the circuit had provided in its original incarnation. The work to renovate the track was carried out with enormous care. Surviving wartime buildings were put back to first-class order. Trackside advertising was to be in period-style, and everything was done to recreate both the original circuit and the atmosphere that pervaded it.

Goodwood is said to be the only circuit in England (and possibly much further afield) that has remained unchanged for over 50 years and where drivers of historic racing machinery can really experience 'what it must have been like'.

In the most glorious September weather, the circuit reopened to racing on 18 September 1998, exactly 50 years since it all began.

GOODWOOD – THE PERFECT LAP by TONY BROOKS

Reproduced by kind permission of *Autocar* – first published 20 April 1962

AT Goodwood, on 22 March 1952, I made my debut as a racing driver in my father's blue Healey Silverstone. After five practice laps my heart sank. I thought that if all circuits were as tricky as this one I could not imagine myself progressing very far in the sport.

From that day to this I have had a great respect for Goodwood and its 2.4 miles of challenging motoring. Six of its seven main corners need to be taken in drifts – all four wheels sliding relative to the road – and the adverse cambers, together with the curved approaches to a number of corners, call for the highest qualities in the driver of a powerful car.

Although the Goodwood circuit has been developed from a wartime aerodrome, every effort has been made to create the impression of racing on a road circuit. A compromise has been struck between the circuit where the driver will bend his car, if not himself, should he make the slightest mistake, and the circuit where 'over the limit' motoring is encouraged by wide open spaces.

Goodwood, in addition to making exacting demands on the driver, calls for a very finely balanced car, with first-class roadholding, so that it may be 'thrown around' in the corners with almost gay abandon. Good braking is also at a premium and good healthy horses in the middle of the engine's power curve are needed.

The axle ratio is unusually critical and as maximum revolutions are reached in top for a few fleeting seconds on only two occasions it generally pays to gear the car so that it achieves perhaps 100 or 200rpm more than the figure at which maximum power is produced. Intermediate gears also need to be chosen carefully – a fourth gear to achieve maximum revolutions when about to brake for Madgwick – a third which will suit St Mary's and perhaps be held all the way round to the exit from Lavant corner, yet be able to provide punch to control the back of the car out of Woodcote and accelerate on power to the chicane.

The importance of roadholding is indicated by the fact that the late Peter Collins lapped Goodwood in the V16 1½-litre supercharged BRM, with more than 400bhp, in 1 min 33.0 sec (92.80mph) in 1955, yet last year a Formula Junior with a 1,100 cc unit and around 90bhp took only 1 min 33.4 sec

(92.50 mph) for the same lap. This Junior figure has since been improved upon by R.M. Prior (Lola-Ford) to 1 min 29.0 sec (97.08mph) at the first 1962 Club Meeting. These figures point to the tremendous progress which has been made in racing car design; although the latter meeting was the first to be held on the completely resurfaced circuit, it is certain that the BRM figure would have been improved upon anyway.

It is expected that the new surface will reduce tyre wear considerably and yet provide very good grip in the dry and in the wet. Tyre wear used to be a tremendous problem in the longer races and it is said that the sight of so many worn tyres stacked up behind the pits after the TT caused more than one person to buy large blocks of shares in a certain rubber company.

Even with its new surface, Goodwood will present the same problems to the driver. If you imagine yourself as an experienced driver at the wheel of an Intercontinental 2½-litre car – giving 260bhp and using a five-speed gearbox – at the start of a flying lap, you would go through the following routine:

You cross the start and finish line in fourth gear, accelerating hard towards Madgwick, a long, seemingly never-ending, right-hander. It is really two corners in one, with two apexes, and is taken in one continuous drift when sufficient power is available. The entry to the corner is slightly curved, so you approach it a little to the right of the centre of the road. As you start to brake from around 120mph, after the marshal's hut on the right-hand side of the road, you travel in a straight line towards the left-hand side, finishing the braking with a few feet to spare. As the brakes are released you line the car up on the first apex, and the drift is initiated by pointing the car so that it appears as if it will run over the grass at the apex. The speed of the car – still around 90mph – causes the front wheels to slide as they are pointed along too ambitious a line, and application of the throttle causes the rear wheels to slide producing a four-wheel drift.

The correct amount of drift is maintained by throttle control. You clip the first apex and the car follows a steady arc, drifting out no farther than the centre of the road, so as to avoid an adverse camber. Small steering corrections may be

made to assist the maintenance of the correct angle of drift, but the fewer the better, for on fast corners frequent corrections and fighting with the wheel tend to increase the friction between the tyre and the road.

The sweep takes the car close in at the second apex and you then use more throttle so that the car drifts over to the left-hand side of the road, with the tail coming out a little. A small amount of left lock is applied to reduce the drift as the car assumes the correct angle for maximum acceleration from the corner. This is achieved by balancing the steering correction against the amount of throttle and relating it to the width of road left, the car being allowed to slide within 6 inches of the edge of the road.

You accelerate hard in fourth gear towards Fordwater, a very difficult right-hand sweep in a 2½-litre car but comfortably taken with the accelerator hard on the foot with a Formula 1 car. This is where the top class driver cuts his lap time in a powerful car. You change into fifth a hundred yards before the curve and approach it on the left-hand side of the road. You aim to knock down the flag that marks the apex of the corner, for the road falls away and the exact line cannot be chosen without using an artificial marker.

If the approach line is correct and the drift carries the car close into the flag, you should be able to take the corner in a 125mph drift, but the slightest error in the line will compel you to ease the throttle up and put it down again. The car drifts to the left-hand side of the road at an alarming speed as the adverse camber takes charge, and this must be allowed for. If you have taken the corner 'flat' a higher maximum speed will be achieved before braking for the right-hander before St Mary's, where there is a most difficult curved approach with adverse camber in the braking area. At this point the car touches about 135–140mph, a speed sometimes greater than that achieved on Lavant straight, depending on the wind direction.

You start braking in the centre of the road, by the marker board. Using the heel and toe technique you select fourth gear while the straight line braking takes you to within 10ft of the edge of the road in an area where the adverse camber is minimal. You set the car up in a 90mph drift and clip the greasy apex very close, allowing the car to drift out no farther than the centre of the road, as the left-hander of St Mary's follows immediately afterwards. This must be approached from the right-hand side of the road so the best line on the right-hander has to be sacrificed for St Mary's.

As soon as you have killed the drift after the right-hander, by using a little left lock, you brake hard, select third, and throw the car into the 70mph St Mary's left-hander, the camber again falling away. The throttle is used to balance the car in the drift, with a little steering correction, and the car must be prevented from drifting out wide until the exit is reached, when the power is gently turned on.

You then accelerate hard towards the first part of Lavant corner, and once again a slight right-handed kink prevents a straight approach to the corner. A positive effort to brake in a straight line must be made, starting just after the kink, and finishing up on the extreme left of the circuit. It is another 'two in one' right-hand corner. You clip the first apex very close and immediately start feeding on the power and building up a drift which takes the car in a steady curve, clipping the grass on the left-hand side before it takes you in to touch the grass on the inside at the second apex, at about 75mph. You then really start getting your foot down and the car, continuing its

steady curve, drifts to the left-hand side of the road again and a few seconds later you snatch fourth.

You enter the so-called straight accelerating hard, and the maximum achieved depends on how well you have negotiated Lavant corner. So it is important to make a good exit, even if it means a relatively slow entrance.

At the slight left-hand curve in the straight you change into top. Just before braking into Woodcote corner you touch 140mph, which seems pretty quick as Woodcote, another double apex corner, rushes up. Hard braking as you enter the first kink before Woodcote can unsteady the car if it is the slightest bit overdone, which prevents you ever getting back on to the correct line.

You take third gear while braking and then ignore the apex of the first part of the corner, passing no closer than 6ft to it, in order that your drifting sweep, starting immediately after the braking has stopped, may take you over to almost touch the left-hand side of the road. At this point you turn on more power to set up a broader drift to get the back of the car round for the relatively sharp final part of Woodcote and you clip the grass on the inside at about 70mph. As you do so two bumps tend to unsettle the car, but you keep the power on and use corrective lock if necessary. The wide and late approach enables you to turn the power on

immediately the apex is reached, as the car is already pointing in the right direction, with the back well round.

A short, sharp, burst of acceleration in third gear takes you to the braking point for the chicane on the left-hand side of the road, which used to be marked by a crack in the road before the new surface was laid. This is not a place to risk locking the wheels, as the main part of the chicane is solid brick and there is no room to recover, a relatively slow entrance paying off as it enables the car to be correctly placed for a rapid exit.

Again it is important to get the back of the car well round as you reach the left-hand apex, which is done with the positioning of the car. The power may then be immediately turned on, using second gear, and the rear wheel power slide is controlled largely by steering correction, as it is a slow corner taken at about 35mph. A good exit can affect the lap time to a surprising degree and as you accelerate away and take third, then fourth in front of the pits, you sweep on towards the start of your next lap, having taken about 1 min 25 sec for the lap completed – if you were trying fairly hard.

With cars having surplus power, passing is not as difficult as the succession of corners might suggest, for the careful application of power, and the employment of a drift technique that positions the car correctly for quick exits, enable a driver to out-accelerate another car from a corner. This is especially practicable out of Madgwick, Fordwater, and Lavant corners, and out-braking another driver into Madgwick, Lavant, and Woodcote are other popular means of passing.

The technique with a 1½-litre Grand Prix car is similar to the one described but there is less power available, less drifting, and therefore fewer opportunities to pass, but the maximum speeds of the new cars are probably only about 7mph slower than the 2½-litre cars on such a course.

Goodwood will again renew its challenge to the drivers on Easter Monday. With the help of the new surface, a winter's development, new engines, and keen competition, the Formula 1 cars could well strike another blow for progress and better, by a clear margin, the absolute Intercontinental record of 1 min 24.6 sec (102.13mph), established by Stirling Moss (Cooper) in 1960.

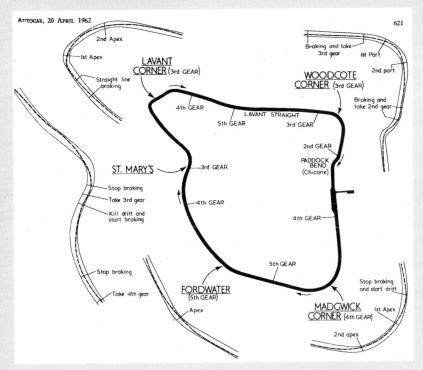

Autocar, 20 April 1962   621

2nd Apex
1st Apex
Straight line braking
LAVANT CORNER (3rd GEAR)
4th GEAR
Braking and take 3rd gear   1st Part
2nd part
WOODCOTE CORNER (3rd GEAR)
Braking and take 2nd gear
LAVANT STRAIGHT
5th GEAR   3rd GEAR
2nd GEAR
PADDOCK BEND (Chicane)
ST. MARY'S   3rd GEAR
4th GEAR
4th GEAR
Stop braking
Take 3rd gear
Kill drift and start braking
Stop braking
Take 4th gear
FORDWATER (5th GEAR)
Apex
5th GEAR
Stop braking and start drift
MADGWICK CORNER (4th GEAR)   1st Apex
2nd apex

Appendix

Results

What follows is a list of the winners of all the races at the Goodwood public meetings. For more detailed results, including those of the Members' Meetings, see *The Glory of Goodwood* by Mike Lawrence, Simon Taylor and Doug Nye (Virgin Books, 1999). For the performance of every entry in every race see *A Record of Motor Racing at Goodwood* by Robert Barker (St Leonards Press, 1999).

18 September 1948: Opening Meeting
Paul Pycroft (Pycroft Jaguar SS100) 66.42mph
Harry Lester (MG L-type Magna) 64.88mph
George Phillips (MG TC) 62.82mph
Ken Watkins (BMW 328) 62.79mph
Stirling Moss (Cooper JAP T2) 71.92mph
Dudley Folland (MG K3) 74.29mph
Dennis Poore (Alfa Romeo 8C/35) 77.74mph
Reg Parnell (Maserati 4CLT) 80.56mph

18 April 1949: Easter Meeting
Dudley Folland (Ferrari 166) 78.03mph
Stan Coldham (Cooper JAP II) 70.80mph
Reg Parnell (Maserati 4CLT) 82.98mph
Frank Kennington (Cisitalia D45) 74.79mph
Reg Parnell (Maserati 4CLT) 82.87mph
Stirling Moss (Cooper JAP T9) 79.76mph
Reg Parnell (Maserati 4CLT) 84.18mph

17 September 1949: September Meeting
Stirling Moss (Cooper JAP T9) 82.10mph
Reg Parnell (Maserati 4CLT) 85.11mph
Peter Collins (Cooper Norton III) 74.95mph
Ken McAlpine (Maserati 8CM) 83.14mph
Tony Rolt (Alfa Romeo Aitken) 83.49mph
Gordon Shillito (Riley) 80.99mph
Reg Parnell (Maserati 4CLT) 86.43mph
Gerry Dunham (Alvis 12-70 Special) 71.15mph

10 April 1950: Easter Meeting
Bill Aston (Cooper JAP T9) 78.92mph
Curly Dryden (Cooper Norton II) 68.40mph
'B Bira' (Maserati 4CLT) 80.63mph
Bill Aston (Cooper JAP T9) 73.77mph
Reg Parnell (Maserati 4CLT) 78.26mph
Gerry Dunham (Alvis 12-70 Special) 69.30mph
Duncan Hamilton (Maserati 6CM) 76.35mph

27 May 1950: Whitsun Meeting
Eric Brandon (Cooper JAP) 75.92mph
Curly Dryden (Cooper Norton) 75.24mph
Basil da Lissa (MG K3) 73.00mph
Gerry Ruddock (HRG) 71.95mph

Curly Dryden (Cooper Norton) 77.23mph
Basil da Lissa (MG K3) 76.06mph

30 September 1950: September Meeting
Bill Aston (Cooper JAP T12) 73.70mph
Curly Dryden (Cooper JAP) 70.75mph
Reg Parnell (BRM T15) 78.50mph
Horace Richards (Riley Nine) 64.50mph
Duncan Hamilton (Maserati 6CM) 75.80mph
Harry Schell (Cooper JAP T9) 72.51mph
Gordon Shillito (Riley) 72.90mph
Reg Parnell (BRM T15) 82.48mph

26 March 1951: Easter Meeting
Stirling Moss (HWM Alta) 80.91mph
Alf Bottoms (JBS Norton) 75.92mph
Reg Parnell (Maserati 4CLT) 82.92mph
Peter Collins (Cooper JAP T12) 81.24mph
John Cooper (Cooper JAP T12) 83.99mph
'B Bira' (OSCA G-4500) 87.57mph
Len Gibbs (HRG Lightweight) 72.85mph
Johnny Claes (Talbot-Lago T26C) 86.50mph

14 April 1951: Motor Cycling's Goodwood Saturday
Maurice Cann (Moto Guzzi) 74.04mph
Les Dear (AJS) 79.24mph
K.R.V. James (BSA) 70.51mph
George Brown (Vincent) 82.84mph
M.C. Tomkinson (Velocette) 66.61mph
Geoff Duke (Norton) 87.07mph
Bill Boddice (Norton) 73.20mph
Geoff Duke (Norton) 83.56mph
C. Lawrence (HRD) 73.82mph

14 May 1951: Whitsun Meeting
Eric Brandon (Cooper Norton V) 80.16mph
Alan Brown (Cooper Norton V) 78.63mph
Reg Parnell (ThinWall Special) 90.07mph
'B Bira' (OSCA G-4500) 88.28mph
Stirling Moss (Kieft Norton) 82.82mph
Reg Parnell (ThinWall Special) 91.64mph

29 September 1951: September Meeting
Stirling Moss (HWM Alta) 84.83mph
Giuseppe Farina (Alfa Romeo 158) 94.83mph
Stirling Moss (Jaguar C-type) 83.67mph
Ken Wharton (Cromard Special) 81.97mph
Stirling Moss (Jaguar C-type) 84.16mph
Giuseppe Farina (Alfa Romeo 158) 94.50mph
Mike Keen (HRG F2) 80.91mph
Giuseppe Farina (Alfa Romeo 158) 95.11mph

14 April 1952: Easter Meeting
Mike Hawthorn (Cooper Bristol T20) 83.18mph
Stirling Moss (Kieft Norton) 78.07mph
Mike Hawthorn (Cooper Bristol T20) 85.43mph
Bill Holt (Jaguar XK120) 75.56mph
Alan Brown (Cooper Bristol T20) 82.15mph
Duncan Hamilton (Talbot-Lago T26C) 84.67mph
Eric Thompson (Aston Martin DB2) 76.34mph
Jose Froilan Gonzalez (ThinWall Special) 88.23mph

4 June 1952: Whitsun Meeting
Bob Gerard (Cooper Norton) 76.94mph
Don Parker (Kieft Norton) 75.29mph
John de Edwards (Healey Silverstone) 70.67mph
Bill Lamb (Healey Silverstone) 73.50mph
Bob Gerard (Cooper Norton) 77.98mph
Mike Hawthorn (Cooper Bristol T20) 85.13mph

16 August 1952: Nine Hours Race
Peter Collins/Pat Griffith (Aston Martin DB3) 75.42mph

27 September 1952: September Meeting
Ken Downing (Connaught A) 84.80mph
Stirling Moss (Cooper Norton) 79.24mph
Jose Froilan Gonzalez (BRM T15) 87.64mph
Tony Rolt (Jaguar C-type) 83.62mph
Tony Gaze (Maserati 8CM) 82.82mph
Bill Dobson (Jaguar XK120) 77.76mph
Jose Froilan Gonzalez (BRM T15) 88.13mph

7 April 1953: Easter Meeting
Joe Goodhew (Darracq T150C) 74.10mph
Baron E. de Graffenried (Maserati A6GCM) 87.63mph
Alan Brown (Cooper Norton VIIa) 80.97mph
Ron Flockhart (ERA D-type) 85.46mph
Baron E. de Graffenried (Maserati A6GCM) 79.48mph
Jimmy Stewart (Cooper Bristol T20) 80.22mph
Cliff Davis (Tojeiro Bristol) 76.19mph
Ken Wharton (BRM T15) 90.47mph

22 August 1953: Nine Hours Race
Reg Parnell/Eric Thompson (Aston Martin DB3S) 78.94mph

26 September 1953: September Meeting
Roy Salvadori (Connaught A) 89.63mph
George Abecassis (HWM Jaguar) 83.00mph
Mike Hawthorn (ThinWall Special) 92.11mph
Don Parker (Kieft Norton) 81.36mph
Mike Hawthorn (ThinWall Special) 92.70mph
Peter Woozley (Allard J2X) 75.52mph
Graham Whitehead (ERA C-type) 85.42mph

19 April 1954: Easter Meeting
Reg Parnell (Ferrari 500/625) 88.77mph
Jimmy Stewart (Jaguar C-type) 82.11mph
Ken Wharton (BRM P30) 88.70mph
Tony Crook (Cooper Bristol T24) 81.50mph
Tony Rolt (Connaught A-type) 87.28mph
Les Leston (Cooper Norton) 82.19mph
Claude Hamilton (ERA B-type) 78.46mph
Ken Wharton (BRM T15) 86.40mph

7 June 1954: Whitsun Meeting
Reg Bicknell (Revis Norton) 81.66mph
Reg Parnell (Ferrari 500/625) 87.63mph
Jimmy Stewart (Jaguar C-type) 85.52mph
Peter Collins (ThinWall Special) 91.53mph
Sir Jeremy Boles (Aston Martin DB3) 76.06mph
Desmond Titterington (Triumph TR2) 70.99mph

25 September 1954: September Meeting
Bob Gerard (Cooper Bristol T23) 86.89mph
Don Parker (Kieft Norton) 81.39mph
Roy Salvadori (Maserati A6GCS) 82.13mph
Stirling Moss (Maserati 250F) 91.49mph
Roy Salvadori (Jaguar C-type) 83.88mph
Peter Collins (ThinWall Special) 92.07mph
Noel Berrow Johnson (Martin Norton) 78.52mph

11 April 1955: Easter Meeting
Roy Salvadori (Connaught A-type) 86.57mph
Les Leston (Connaught AL/SR) 81.66mph
Peter Collins (BRM P30) 90.29mph
Ivor Bueb (Cooper Norton) 82.13mph
Roy Salvadori (Aston Martin DB3S) 83.40mph
Archie Scott Brown (Lister Bristol) 83.06mph
Roy Salvadori (Maserati 250F) 89.26mph
Bob Gerard (Cooper Bristol T23) 88.25mph

30 May 1955: Whitsun Meeting
Colin Chapman (Lotus MG Mk IX) 81.75mph
Mike Anthony (Lotus Bristol Mk X) 82.83mph
Duncan Hamilton (Jaguar D-type) 83.72mph
John Tozer (Amilcar C6) 72.26mph
Nancy Mitchell (Daimler Conquest) 64.57mph
Richard Murdoch (Rolls Royce 20/25) 49.27mph
Duncan Hamilton (Jaguar D-type) 84.41mph

20 August 1955: Nine Hours Race
Peter Walker/Dennis Poore (Aston Martin
    DB3S) 82.24mph

2 April 1956: Easter Meeting
Roy Salvadori (Cooper Climax T39) 87.17mph
Ivor Bueb (Cooper Norton) 83.24mph
Stirling Moss (Aston Martin DB3S) 89.18mph
Roy Salvadori (Cooper Climax T39) 86.30mph
Stirling Moss (Maserati 250F) 94.35mph
Ken Rudd (AC Bristol) 78.84mph
Ron Flockhart (Jaguar D-type) 86.77mph

21 May 1956: Whitsun Meeting
Colin Chapman (Lotus Climax 11) 85.88mph
Jim Russell (Cooper Norton) 82.14mph
Bob Berry (Jaguar D-type) 87.85mph
Desmond Titterington (Jaguar D-type) 87.65mph
Barry Eastick (Bentley) 67.21mph

8 September 1956: September Meeting
Keith Hall (Lotus Climax 11) 84.62mph
Jim Russell (Cooper Norton) 83.33mph
Roy Salvadori (Cooper Climax T41) 88.34mph
Alan Stacey (Lotus Climax 11) 82.76mph
Roy Salvadori (Cooper Climax T41) 89.07mph
Tony Brooks (Aston Martin DB3S) 88.19mph
Jock Lawrence (Jaguar D-type) 84.44mph

22 April 1957: Easter Meeting
Ken Rudd (AC Bristol) 79.66mph
Tony Brooks (Cooper Climax T41) 88.84mph
Colin Chapman (Lotus Climax 11) 87.32mph
Stuart Lewis-Evans (Connaught B-type)
    90.66mph
Archie Scott Brown (Lister Jaguar) 89.42mph
Stuart Lewis-Evans (Beart Cooper Norton)
    83.14mph

10 June 1957: Whitsun Meeting
John Sprinzel (Austin A35) 62.65mph
Alan Stacey (Lotus Climax 11) 83.18mph
Donald Day (Bentley) 65.11mph
Michael Head (Cooper Jaguar T38) 85.88mph
Avril Scott-Moncrieff (Lotus MG Mk VI)
    68.27mph
Paul Fletcher (AC Ace) 75.62mph

28 September 1957: September Meeting
Stuart Lewis-Evans (Beart Cooper Norton)
    85.70mph
Alan Stacey (Lotus Climax 11) 87.01mph
Roy Salvadori (Cooper Climax T43) 94.42mph
Archie Scott Brown (Lister Jaguar) 88.84mph
John Dalton (Austin Healey 100/6) 76.72mph
Patsy Burt (Cooper Climax T39) 79.33mph

7 April 1958: Easter Meeting
Stuart Lewis-Evans (Beart Cooper Norton)
    83.62mph

Jack Brabham (Cooper Climax T43) 93.76mph
Stirling Moss (Aston Martin DBR2) 89.94mph
Mike Hawthorn (Ferrari Dino 246) 94.96mph
John Campbell-Jones (Lotus Climax 11)
    87.08mph

26 May 1958: Whitsun Meeting
Ted Whiteaway (AC Bristol) 78.36mph
Bill Moss (ERA B-type) 82.14mph
Graham Whitehead (Lister Jaguar) 84.41mph
Jack Sears (Austin Healey 100/6) 76.70mph
Duncan Hamilton (Jaguar 3.4) 78.95mph
Bruce Halford (Lister Jaguar) 87.33mph

13 September 1958: RAC Tourist Trophy
Stirling Moss/Tony Brooks (Aston Martin
    DBR1) 88.83mph

30 March 1959: Easter Meeting
Peter Ashdown (Lola Climax Mk 1) 87.89mph
Jack Brabham (Cooper Climax T45) 93.34mph
Ivor Bueb (Lister Jaguar) 78.64mph
Stirling Moss (Cooper Climax T51) 90.31mph
Ivor Bueb (Jaguar 3.4) 78.40mph

18 May 1959: Whitsun Meeting
Peter Lumsden (Lotus Elite) 79.48mph
Douglas Hull (ERA B-type) 79.69mph
Ron Flockhart (Tojeiro Jaguar) 88.51mph
Syd Hurrell (Triumph TR3) 79.31mph
Richard Utley (Lotus Climax 11) 82.90mph
Paul Fletcher (MGA t/c) 77.42mph

5 September 1959: RAC Tourist Trophy
Stirling Moss/Jack Fairman/Carroll Shelby
    (Aston Martin DBR1)

18 April 1960: Easter Meeting
Jim Clark (Lotus Ford 18) 90.47mph
Innes Ireland (Lotus Climax 18) 96.41mph
Roy Salvadori (Cooper Climax T49) 89.96mph
Innes Ireland (Lotus Climax 18) 100.39mph
Stirling Moss (Aston Martin DB4GT)
    83.03mph

6 June 1960: Whitsun Meeting
Paddy Gaston (Austin A40) 72.91mph
Julian Sutton (Austin Healey) 78.47mph
Tom Dickson (Cooper Climax T49) 88.46mph
Joe Goodhew (ERA Delage) 78.62mph
Colin Hextall (Triumph TR2) 78.94mph
Chris Kerrison (Lotus Climax 11) 84.33mph

20 August 1960: RAC Tourist Trophy
Trevor Taylor (Lotus Ford 18) 90.27mph
Jim Clark (Lotus Ford 18) 89.57mph
Trevor Taylor (Lotus Ford 18) 90.68mph
Stirling Moss (Ferrari 250 GT SWB) 85.58mph

3 April 1961: Easter Meeting
Mike Parkes (Jaguar 3.8) 76.30mph
Stirling Moss (Cooper Climax T53) 90.47mph
Peter Arundell (Lotus Ford 20) 85.08mph
John Surtees (Cooper Climax T53) 95.76mph
Stirling Moss (Lotus Climax 19) 81.57mph
Mike Parkes (Ferrari 250GT SWB) 83.22mph

22 May 1961: Whitsun Meeting
Bob Jankel (Ford Anglia) 75.66mph
Angus Hyslop (Lotus Ford 20) 88.85mph
Bruce Halford (Cooper Climax T49)
  90.05mph
Bob Staples (AC Bristol) 79.82mph
Hon Patrick Lindsay (ERA B-type) 79.54mph
Gordon Jones (Marcos Climax) 80.54mph
Dizzy Addicott (Lotus Climax 11) 81.67mph

19 August 1961: RAC Tourist Trophy
Frank Gardner (Lotus Ford 20) 90.51mph
Alan Rees (Lotus Ford 20) 90.89mph
Alan Rees (Lotus Ford 20) 91.20mph
Stirling Moss (Ferrari 250GT SWB) 86.62mph

23 April 1962: Easter Meeting
Graham Hill (Jaguar 3.8) 86.59mph
Bruce McLaren (Cooper Climax T55)
  99.05mph
Peter Arundell (Lotus Ford 22) 96.04mph
Graham Hill (BRM P578) 102.65mph
Innes Ireland (Lotus Climax 19) 95.50mph

11 June 1962: Whitsun Meeting
Peter Woodroffe (Jaguar 3.8) 81.85mph
Keith Francis (Lotus Ford 20) 92.29mph
Jimmy Blumer (Cooper Climax T49)
  90.98mph
Bill Jones (Morgan +4) 80.44mph
Gordon Chapman (ERA A-type) 82.86mph
George Naylor (Elva BMC Mk 6) 84.94mph
Lord Clydesdale (Lola Climax Mk 1) 85.43mph

18 August 1962: RAC Tourist Trophy
David Cole (Lotus Ford 7) 85.07mph
Peter Arundell (Lotus Ford 22) 98.00mph
Innes Ireland (Ferrari 250GTO) 94.05mph

15 April 1963: Easter Meeting
Frank Gardner (Brabham Ford BT6) 89.68mph
Graham Hill (Jaguar 3.8) 85.02mph
Innes Ireland (Lotus BRM 24) 102.44mph
Graham Hill (Jaguar E-type) 96.62mph
Roy Salvadori (Cooper Climax T61M) 84.14mph

3 June 1963: Whitsun Meeting
Mike Salmon (Jaguar 3.8) 85.77mph
Peter Waller (ERA B-type) 76.62mph
Mike Parkes (Ferrari 250GTO) 86.81mph

Bill de Selincourt (Lotus Climax 19) 89.10mph
John Dangerfield (Morgan +4) 80.90mph
Peter Sutcliffe (Aston Martin DB3S Coupe)
  86.07mph

24 August 1963: RAC Tourist Trophy
Peter Arundell (Lotus Ford 27) 99.18mph
Graham Hill (Ferrari 250GTO) 95.14mph

30 March 1964: Easter Meeting
Jackie Stewart (Cooper Austin T72) 92.47mph
Jack Sears (Ford Galaxie) 89.26mph
Jim Clark (Lotus Climax 25) 104.91mph
Graham Hill (Ferrari 250GTO/64) 96.76mph
John Coundley (Lotus Climax 19) 97.26mph

18 May 1964: Whitsun Meeting
Roger Mac (Brabham Ford BT6) 91.37mph
Jonty Williamson (Bentley) 74.43mph
Roy Salvadori (Cooper Maserati T61P)
  96.15mph
Bob Olthoff (Ford Cortina GT) 86.03mph
Bill Wilks (Cooper Bristol T20) 82.51mph
Mike Cox (Austin A40) 78.06mph

29 August 1964: RAC Tourist Trophy
Mike Spence (Lotus Elan) 92.76mph
Graham Hill (Ferrari 330P) 97.13mph

19 April 1965: Easter Meeting
Roy Pike (Brabham Ford BT16) 88.42mph
Jim Clark (Lotus Cortina) 79.85mph
Jim Clark (Lotus Climax 25) 105.07mph
Roger Mac (AC Cobra) 95.70mph
Jim Clark (Lotus Ford 30) 103.44mph

7 June 1965: Whitsun Meeting
Piers Courage (Brabham Ford BT10) 95.87mph
Bob Salvage (Connaught A-type) 81.94mph
John Coundley (McLaren Elva Olds M1A)
  98.67mph
Mike Salmon (Ford Mustang) 88.00mph
John Sparrow (AC Cobra) 92.51mph

11 April 1966: Easter Meeting
Chris Irwin (Brabham Ford BT18) 97.94mph
Brian Muir (Ford Galaxie) 91.25mph
Jack Brabham (Brabham Honda BT18)
  102.79mph
John Miles (Lotus Elan) 92.14mph
Mike Spence (Parnell BRM) 97.78mph

30 May 1966: Whitsun Meeting
Chris Lawrence (Morgan SLR) 87.83mph
Alan Peer (Ford Anglia) 87.76mph)
David Cole (Brabham Ford BT18) 96.29mph
Tony Dean (Brabham Climax BT8) 94.20mph
Peter Brewer (Aston Martin DBR4) 84.54mph

Index